Famous Phrases
from the Bible

D1494247

B BIBLE
SOCIETY

The British and Foreign Bible Society
Stonehill Green
Westlea
Swindon
SN5 7DG

Famous Phrases from the Bible © 2011 Bible Society
ISBN 978-0-564-04766-6

Scriptures quotations are from the
King James Authorised Version.

Rights in the Authorised Version of the Bible in
the United Kingdom are vested in the Crown. Published
in the United Kingdom by permission of the Crown's
patentee, Cambridge University Press.

Illustrations by Horace Knowles © 1954, 1967, 1972, 2011
The British and Foreign Bible Society. Additions and
amendments by Louise Bass © 1994 The British and Foreign
Bible Society.

Classic Phrases © 2011 Crossref-it; adapted from
'A–Z: Common sayings from the Bible' published by
Crossref-it on www.crossref-it.info

Typography and typesetting by
Bible Society Resources Ltd, a wholly-owned subsidiary of
The British and Foreign Bible Society

Cover design by
Patrick Knowles

Production arranged by
Bible Society Resources Ltd

visit
biblesociety.org.uk
bibleresources.org.uk

Printed in the United Kingdom

KJV/BSR/2011/8.5M

Introduction

I was delighted to be asked to introduce this publication. But I have to admit that I am always tempted to leave the actual writing to the eleventh hour. And, having once set my hand to the plough, I needed to fight the good fight, gird my loins, and get on with exploring the influence of the Bible on English, going through fire and water if necessary. I realised if I did not, that I could be found wanting and have to apologise, in sackcloth and ashes, for failing to count the cost. The fly in the ointment, of course, is that the flesh is weak and there are plenty of things that could deflect me from the straight and narrow way: perhaps not quite the fleshpots of Egypt, but a temptation to hide my light under a bushel; I confess I have feet of clay, and there have been times when I have wanted to wash my hands of the whole thing. That's a cross I have to bear.

If you have the patience of Job and have read this far, I hope it has not set your teeth on edge. In the preceding sentences, I have used eighteen biblical or Bible-related idioms, and when they are clustered in this fashion, they may seem a little incongruous. In other contexts we often use idioms deriving from the Bible, and the King James Bible in particular, with little sense of that origin. Some time ago I came across an item in the British tabloid newspaper, the *Daily Mail*, which publishes a fascinating 'Notes and Queries' column. Questions sent in by readers are answered by other readers or experts of various kinds. A question was asked (Thursday 1 March, 2001, p. 77), 'Where does the saying "by the skin of your teeth" come from?' This was the answer published:

> *This expression seems strange, but in 1953 Scientific American reported: 'Microscopic techniques now reveal tooth enamel to be not a dead shell but the strongest tissue in the body — a 'superskin'.*
>
> *The enamel is produced by skin (epithelial) cells. The enamel is not fixed or dead. Like other hard tissues it carries on a traffic with its environment, albeit without the aid of blood vessels or cells.' So the skin of the teeth may be much stronger than once thought.*

An excellent answer to the question 'what is the skin of the teeth?', and fascinating in itself. But it does not quite show where the saying came from. The answer to that is Job 19.20 of the King James Version (KJV) of the Bible, which reads, 'My bone cleaveth to my skin and to my flesh, And I am escaped with the skin of my teeth.'

In this passage Job is lamenting the dreadful miseries that have befallen him: the loss of his family, friends, possessions and health. At this point in the story he feels he is losing himself, as his body wastes away. He is barely alive. In the Hebrew of this passage, it is possible that 'the skin of the teeth' means the gums; that is, Job's teeth have fallen out. Job is alive, but only just: he has escaped death, so far, 'with the skin of his teeth', but not with his actual teeth. We use the saying now to talk about desperate or terrifying near-miss situations: when we only just manage to do something, or narrowly miss death or serious injury.

This saying is not known to have been used in English before the publication of the Geneva Bible in 1560 and it was later taken up and popularised by the KJV in 1611, and it illustrates very neatly the influence of these works. We use the saying without consciousness of its origin, or indeed of its original meaning. Yet we use it in a way that is quite close to that original meaning. The saying has filtered through centuries of use and has become part of the rich idiomatic resources of English. Learners of English as a foreign language find this aspect of English one of the hardest to understand and master, because the meaning of idioms like this one is often at variance with a surface, literal sense. The science of the answer about 'the skin of the teeth' is no doubt correct, but it scarcely begins to answer the question about the saying and its origin.

The Bible in English

There have been many books about the translation of the Bible into English, and the 400th anniversary of the King James Bible has encouraged the production of a good crop, one of the best of which is Gordon Campbell's *Bible: the Story of the King James Version, 1611–2011* (Oxford: Oxford University Press, 2010). What emerges from even the briefest glance at the history of English translations of the Bible is that from the very beginnings of Christianity in England, it was a book which was 'most necessary for all people to know' — these words taken from King Alfred (reigned 871–899), who himself translated at least some of the Psalms into Old English.

The Bible for King Alfred and his predecessors was the Latin Vulgate, a translation made largely by St Jerome from the original Hebrew and Greek at the end of the fourth century and into the fifth. The Vulgate was the Bible of the western Middle Ages, and was within limits a very good translation; and as its name suggests, it was originally a Bible for the masses. That simple notion that was somewhat complicated by the expansion of Christianity into non-Latin-speaking Germanic lands like England. And in the years after the Norman Conquest the inaccessibilty of the language of the Latin Bible to ordinary people was a means of reinforcing the power of the political and religious hierarchy over secular and spiritual life.

John Wyclif (and his followers) translated parts of the Vulgate in the 1380s. For this crime Wyclif was condemned for heresy and his bones were dug up and burnt after his death. William Tyndale was hounded by the authorities for his translation work on the Bible and he was executed in 1536. Both Tyndale and Miles Coverdale (whose translation of the whole Bible was published in 1535) did most of their translation work and publishing on the continent because of this opposition in England. And indeed they drew on the scholarship of continental scholars such as Erasmus, who had edited the Greek New Testament earlier in the sixteenth century, and Luther, who had translated the Bible into German. The Geneva Bible was also, as its name suggests, a continental production, published in 1560 at the height of the Reformation and from a decidedly Protestant perspective; it had commentary and annotations in the margins to help the reader. When in due course the authorities in England adopted Protestantism, the Catholic Bible translators in turn had to work in exile on the continent. The Douai-Rheims version based on the Latin Vulgate, was produced and published on the continent, the New Testament in 1582, the Old in 1609.

This history alerts us to the fact that Bible translation in English was always much more than an insular, parochial affair. It touched not merely on matters linguistic, but also and more importantly on spiritual, social, educational and political issues; and it involved views of the Christian church which transcended nationality. Opposition to Bible translation in England was partly due to fear of anarchy and loss of control, but partly also to reverence for tradition and order. When it became increasingly clear in the sixteenth century that the Bible was being widely used in translations of various kinds, approved versions were produced by the bishops: the Great Bible (1539) and the Bishops' Bible (1572) were the more important ones. But the great achievement of the committee established in 1604 under the authority of King James was to produce a Bible translation that addressed most of the issues that had caused difficulty before. It was based on the best translations available (especially Tyndale) and the best manuscripts known of the original languages; it was close to being theologically neutral, neither Protestant nor Catholic; it was conservative and decorous in language; and it was 'appointed to be read in churches' by the highest authority in the land. Its influence on language, literature, imagination and behaviour has been enormous.

The Bible and English

As the anecdote with which I started shows, the influence of the Bible is not always readily recognised by people today. The present booklet springs from the Cross Reference Project, sponsored by Bible Society, which has the aim of making this heritage in language, literature and culture clear and accessible. It contains extracts from one of a number of resources, available either online (crossref-it. info) or in print, produced for use by teachers and pupils in schools today. The booklet outlines the meaning and usage, as well as indicating the sources of just a few of the idioms of present-day English that derive from the Bible. It can, and I hope will, be enjoyed just for the information it gives. But as part of the bigger project, it highlights the wealth and quality of the material available.

In what remains of this introduction, I would like to sketch out some areas of biblical influence in English that might otherwise escape notice. I make no claims to comprehensiveness, and there is an increasing wealth of research in the areas I mention, but it may be interesting to the casual reader to have some indication of the nooks and crannies, as well the broad plains, of biblical influence.

Proverbs

English is rich in biblical proverbs and proverbial phrases. Proverbial phrases are usually simple comparisons like 'bold as a lion' or 'hungry as a hunter'. Others are fixed expressions like 'far be it from me' (2 Samuel 20.20), or to 'set one's face against' something (Leviticus 17.10 and often). It is not always easy to be certain where these phrases derive from, of course, but the influence of the Bible is often marked. 'Bold as a lion' might seem a pretty obvious simile. But before the seventeenth century, we find hardy, stern, proud, fierce, and particularly valiant, as lion-like characteristics, but not bold. The whole proverb in Proverbs 28.1 gives the context for the phrase: 'The wicked flee when no man pursueth: but the righteous are bold as a lion'. Bold is a particularly good adjective in this context because the proverb is talking not about what the lion does or even looks like, but about its air of confidence, its whole demeanor, and the writer contrasts the deep-seated fear of the wicked with the confidence of the righteous.

'Hungry as a hunter', I suspect, derives from the biblical story of Jacob and Esau in Genesis 25. Esau was so desperately hungry after his hunting that he gave up his rights as his father's heir in return for some food his brother Jacob had ready. But the proverbial phrase is not recorded before the end of the sixteenth century, and any explicit connection it might have had with the biblical story has been lost. In this case the proverbial phrase has probably become generalised, that is, it has lost its specific reference to the story and to the moral disapproval the story implies, as it has been used. It now simply refers to the insatiable pangs that this vigorous pastime gives, or gave, rise to.

This last example alerts us to the fact that proverbs and proverbial phrases undergo a whole range of processes in use. 'Spare the rod and spoil the child' derives from

Proverbs 13.24, found in the KJB as 'he that spareth his rod hateth his son: But he that loveth him chasteneth him betimes'. What the current form of the proverb does is to pare away the pronouns and reduce the whole to simple words, so we have an almost perfectly polished monosyllabic, balanced, alliterating saying. The proverb has in fact long outlived the school of educational thought that produced it.

Words

It is not only idioms and proverbs that come to us from the Bible. Some remarkably useful words were first used in biblical translations. The *Oxford English Dictionary* (oed.com) gives the first recorded example of a current word, 'birthright', from Miles Coverdale's 1535 translation of Genesis 25.31, where Jacob demands the rights of the firstborn from his ravenous brother Esau in return for some food. William Tyndale is attributed with the invention of the word 'scapegoat' in his translation of Leviticus 16.8 of 1530, where the word refers to a goat onto which the sins of the people were transferred by the ritual of laying hands on its head, and which was then led into the desert and set free. We still scapegoat people (the verb is relatively recent, first recorded in 1943), essentially blaming the blameless. The OED attributes the sense development of the word 'talent', originally a unit of weight, to refer to a person's skills or gifts and abilities, to the parable of the talents in Matthew 25.14–30. These words did not originate in the King James Bible, but the translators recognised their usefulness and appropriateness and unhesitatingly adopted them.

Literature

The literary influence of the Bible is widespread. It is impossible to even scratch the surface of literary references to the Bible, such is the quantity of them, even in titles alone, so I will content myself by referring the enquirer to Dee Dyas and Esther Hughes, *The Bible in Western Culture: The Student's Guide* (London: Routledge, 2005) for references to art, literature and music. I will, however, add just a few idiosyncratic examples.

Beulah, found in the Bible only at Isaiah 62.4, was popularised as the pleasant land surrounding the City of Gold, the destination of the pilgrims in both parts of John Bunyan's *Pilgrim's Progress* (1678 and 1684). The Land of Nod (used as a place-name in Yorkshire and referred to in the text below) was 'east of Eden', the latter becoming the title of a novel by John Steinbeck (1952); the title of his novel, *To a God Unknown* (1933), makes reference to Acts 17.23, and his apocalyptic *The Grapes of Wrath* (1939) continues the biblical theme in titles, abbreviated from Revelation 14.19.

In Anthony Trollope's Barsetshire novels, the Rector of Puddingdale is Mr Quiverful, first introduced in chapter 19 of *The Warden* (1855). Victorian and earlier novelists tended to use names rather heavy-handedly in characterisation, but this reference to Psalm 127.5, where children are likened to arrows, gently tells us something about Mr Quiverful's situation beyond the fact that he has many children (twelve, in fact) — his impecuniosity and busyness, perhaps. A search on the internet reveals that there is a movement in America today called Quiverfull which opposes birth control.

Bible influence does not only appear in 'high' literature. I remember as a youth singing songs around a campfire, of which an enduringly popular one began,

> *My eyes are dim I cannot see*
> *I have not brought my specs with me...*

While the second and subsequent lines were subject to scabrously inventive variations, the first line remained constant: 'his eyes were dim, [so] that he could not see' is recorded of Isaac in Genesis 27.1, Jacob (Israel) in Genesis 48.10 and Eli in 1 Samuel 4.15.

And finally...

Bible influence is found throughout English culture, and particularly appears in the language, the proverbs, the words and names, as well as the habitual idioms that we use. This booklet helpfully identifies and explains some of the idioms. The Bible translators recognised a neat phrase, a well-turned image, a powerful sentiment, a memorable proverb. The culture for which the Bible was first translated was initially a largely illiterate one, and it was through hearing the Bible read and preached that its impact was first made. With the growth of literacy, the richness of its language became more widely available to the individual. But the English language shows that Bible influence is not restricted to the register of piety and the subject-matter of religion: there is irony and humour, craft and imagination in the application of biblical phrases in the idioms and entertainments of everyday life. Nevertheless, it should be obvious that nobody ever sat down with the Bible to improve their word-skills or find a title for their latest novel. The primary purpose of readers, and the aim of the translators, was to discern the character of God and his purpose for his world. The Bible was one of the books 'most necessary for all people to know'; it had, and continues to have, gifted translators, but its linguistic and cultural impact derives essentially from its profound importance as revelation.

Paul Cavill
School of English Studies
University of Nottingham

a time for everything

Usage: Usually in the context of 'a time [and place] for everything'. The phrase is used to recommend appropriate behaviour and condemn the opposite; also to indicate that something has taken place at an appropriate time, e.g. death.

Context: The biblical context refers to the interlocking movements of history in the individual's life and the nation's: birth and death, war and peace. All of these lie in the power of God.

> **Ecclesiastes 3.1–3**
> *To every thing there is a season, and a time to every purpose under the heaven: a time to be born, and a time to die; a time to plant, and a time to pluck up that which is planted; a time to kill, and a time to heal; a time to break down, and a time to build up.*

Aaron's rod

Usage: A miraculous event serving as a warning or acting as a sign of someone's significance. DH Lawrence's novel of this title (1922) gives his hero's flute (his 'rod') a symbolic significance.

Context: The reference usually is to 'Aaron's rod that budded', Numbers 17.10 and Hebrews 9.4. The miracle was to show that Aaron was God's chosen leader. It was placed in the ark of the covenant as a warning to would-be rebels against God's appointed leaders.

> **Hebrews 9.4**
> *which had the golden censer, and the ark of the covenant overlaid round about with gold, wherein was the golden pot that had manna, and Aaron's rod that budded, and the tables of the covenant.*

Abraham's bosom

Usage: Refers to rest and welcome in heaven for the faithful. Shakespeare uses the proverb in Richard III as a euphemism for death: 'The sons of Edward sleep in Abraham's bosom.'

Context: Abraham was the 'father' of the Jewish and Christian faiths and is believed to be waiting in heaven to receive his 'children in faith'.

> **Luke 16.22**
> *And it came to pass, that the beggar died, and was carried by the angels into Abraham's bosom: the rich man also died, and was buried.*

Absalom

Usage: A byword for a greatly loved family member who repays love with ingratitude and betrayal.

Context: Absalom was King David of Israel's favourite son who rebelled against him and was defeated and killed very much against David's wishes.

> **2 Samuel 18.32–33**
> *And the king said unto Cushi, Is the young man Absalom safe? And Cushi answered, The enemies of my lord the king, and all that rise against thee to do thee hurt, be as that young man is. And the king was much moved, and went up to the chamber over the gate, and wept: and as he went, thus he said, O my son Absalom, my son, my son Absalom! would God I had died for thee, O Absalom, my son, my son!*

Adam's apple

Usage: A feature of the human neck; this lump, or protrusion, is formed by the angle of the thyroid cartilage surrounding the larynx.

Context: The term originates from the story of the Garden of Eden. In the story, God forbade Adam and Eve to touch the fruit of the tree of knowledge. The type of fruit is not mentioned, but is traditionally imagined to be an apple. The 'Adam's apple' is named after the fruit which is supposed to have stuck in Adam's throat.

> **Genesis 2.9**
> *And out of the ground made the LORD God to grow every tree that is pleasant to the sight, and good for food; the tree of life also in the midst of the garden, and the tree of knowledge of good and evil.*

Adam's rib

Usage: Refers to a woman. The feminist magazine *Spare Rib* used the phrase ironically. Women are independent and important in their own right, not just appendages made from and for men as the biblical story seems to imply.

Context: The creation stories in Genesis explain how men and women are jointly made by God for each other and in God's image. The use of the rib means that woman and man are of the same kind and dependent on each other but different from the animals.

> **Genesis 2.21–23**
> *And the LORD God caused a deep sleep to fall upon Adam, and he slept: and he took one of his ribs, and closed up the flesh instead thereof; and the rib, which the LORD God had taken from man, made he a woman, and brought her unto the man. And Adam said, This is now bone of my bones, and flesh of my flesh: she shall be called Woman, because she was taken out of Man.*

Adullam's cave

Usage: A reference to a group set up in opposition to authority.

Context: Refers to the cave where David and his men hid from Saul.

> **1 Samuel 22.1**
> *David therefore departed thence, and escaped to the cave Adullam: and when his brethren and all his father's house heard it, they went down thither to him.*

alien corn

Usage: 'Alien corn' provides the means to live stripped of what makes life worth living. Keats' 'Ode to a Nightingale' refers to 'the sad heart of Ruth when sick for home She stood in tears amid the alien corn' (Ruth 1.66–67).

Context: Ruth, a non-Israelite, gleans (picks up grain missed by the reapers) in order to survive in Israel.

> **Ruth 2.2–3**
> *And Ruth the Moabitess said unto Naomi, Let me now go to the field, and glean ears of corn after him in whose sight I shall find grace. And she said unto her, Go, my daughter. And she went, and came, and gleaned in the field after the reapers: and her hap was to light on a part of the field belonging unto Boaz, who was of the kindred of Elimelech.*

all flesh is grass

Usage: Indicates the fragility and transience of human existence and success.

Context: The rapid growth and flourishing of grass and flowers after rain in Israel and their equally rapid withering in the hot sun is an image of human frailty against which is contrasted the permanence of God's word.

> **1 Peter 1.24–25**
> *For All flesh is as grass, And all the glory of man as the flower of grass. The grass withereth, and the flower thereof falleth away: But the word of the Lord endureth for ever. And this is the word which by the gospel is preached unto you.*

all things to all men

Usage: Usually used to suggest that being 'all things to all men' is impossible, i.e. that one cannot meet the needs, wishes and expectations of everyone; also used of people who try to appeal to everyone.

Context: The apostle Paul made every effort to put no barrier between himself and those with whom he was talking, intending to find common ground so that he could explain his faith in Christ.

1 Corinthians 9.22
To the weak became I as weak, that I might gain the weak: I am made all things to all men, that I might by all means save some.

Alpha and Omega

Usage: The first and last letters of the Greek alphabet so the phrase refers to the beginning and end or the totality of something (or indeed everything).

Context: A name for God, the one who brings creation into being and who will bring the world to an end. The letters were widely used in early Christian art to signify Christ.

Revelation 1.8 see also Revelation 21.6
I am Alpha and Omega, the beginning and the ending, saith the Lord, which is, and which was, and which is to come, the Almighty.

am I my brother's keeper?

Usage: What someone might say when excusing themselves of unwanted responsibility, especially for another person's actions.

Context: Cain had just murdered his brother Abel in a fit of jealous rage but pretended to be ignorant of his whereabouts when challenged by God.

Genesis 4.9
And the LORD said unto Cain, Where is Abel thy brother? And he said, I know not: Am I my brother's keeper?

angel of death

Usage: Refers to an outside force which results in many deaths, e.g. an earthquake or war.

Context: When the Angel of Death passes through to smite the Egyptian first-born, God prevents 'the destroyer' from entering houses with blood on the lintel and side posts. In 2 Kings the 'Angel of the Lord' smites 185,000 men in the Assyrian camp. In the Bible, the fourth horseman of Revelation is called Death and is pictured with Hades following him.

Exodus 12.23 see also 2 Kings 19.35; Revelation 6.8
For the LORD will pass through to smite the Egyptians; and when he seeth the blood upon the lintel, and on the two side posts, the LORD will pass over the door, and will not suffer the destroyer to come in unto your houses to smite you.

apple of one's eye

Usage: Something absolutely precious to the one who has it; often used of a person. The 'apple' is the pupil of the eye.

Context: One instinctively protects one's eyes and this phrase describes God's protection of and love for his people. He expects his people to hold his law equally precious.

> **Deuteronomy 32.10 see also Psalm 17.8; Proverbs 7.2**
> *He found him in a desert land, And in the waste howling wilderness; He led him about, he instructed him, He kept him as the apple of his eye.*

Armageddon

Usage: Used to describe any cataclysmic destructive world event; the battle at the end of the world. The title of a Bruce Willis film (1998) where the world is threatened.

Context: The name refers to the hill of Megiddo in Palestine, where King Josiah was killed in a battle against the Eygptians. In John's vision (Revelation) the armies gather here for a climactic battle of good versus evil and the place name becomes an image of any event which threatens to destroy the world.

> **2 Kings 23.29 see also Revelation 16.16**
> *In his days Pharaoh-nechoh king of Egypt went up against the king of Assyria to the river Euphrates: and king Josiah went against him; and he slew him at Megiddo, when he had seen him.*

as old as the hills

Usage: Exceedingly old, often in reference to people.

Context: The reference is to the idea that someone existed before the inhabitants of the place. It is used in Job as a rhetorical question to ask if someone is older than the first man, and as old as the hills that were there when he first walked on them.

> **Job 15.7**
> *Art thou the first man that was born? Or wast thou made before the hills?*

as you sow so shall you reap

Usage: The idea that at some time a person will get what they deserve or fall victim to their own schemes.

Context: The Bible is full of farming metaphors: this one uses the image of the process of germination to assert that even if they do not appear immediately, bad consequences will follow bad deeds.

Galatians 6.7
Be not deceived; God is not mocked: for whatsoever a man soweth, that shall he also reap.

ashes to ashes

Usage: Sometimes refers to the final breakdown of plans or is a comment about how human life is fragile and short; used in the Burial Service of the Church of England; title of BBC television series; title of a David Bowie song (1980); a play by Harold Pinter.

Context: In the biblical idea humanity has a physical component which is earthly ('dust') and a spiritual component (breath or spirit). At death the dust returns to the earth.

Genesis 3.19
in the sweat of thy face shalt thou eat bread, till thou return unto the ground; for out of it wast thou taken: for dust thou art, and unto dust shalt thou return.

at a venture (Bow)

Usage: A chance occurrence; a shot in the dark.

Context: King Ahab goes into battle in disguise in the hope of not being singled out for attack. He is nevertheless killed by a random arrow shot.

1 Kings 22.34
And a certain man drew a bow at a venture, and smote the king of Israel between the joints of the harness: wherefore he said unto the driver of his chariot, Turn thine hand, and carry me out of the host; for I am wounded.

at death's door

Usage: Usually used of someone who is near to death or has narrowly escaped death. Numerous books and films about near-death experiences have 'Death's Door' in the title.

Context: The Bible often uses concrete images for spiritual concepts. Here, dying is likened to leaving a city or a room through a gate or door.

Job 38.17 see also Psalm 107.18
Have the gates of death been opened unto thee? Or hast thou seen the doors of the shadow of death?

at one's wits' end

Usage: At a loss to know what to do and very worried about the situation.

Context: The passage refers to seamen in a severe storm: they try everything they know but can do nothing.

Psalm 107.27
They reel to and fro, and stagger like a drunken man, And are at their wits' end.

Balaam's ass

Usage: A byword for someone or something that is stubborn in its refusal to pursue a course of action (sometimes for a valid but undisclosed reason).

Context: Balaam is a prophet or 'seer'. The irony here is that the ass sees the angel who opposes Balaam and declares God's message to him, thus usurping the seer's role and making an ass of Balaam.

Numbers 22.27–28
And when the ass saw the angel of the LORD, she fell down under Balaam: and Balaam's anger was kindled, and he smote the ass with a staff. And the LORD opened the mouth of the ass, and she said unto Balaam, What have I done unto thee, that thou hast smitten me these three times?

baptism of fire

Usage: A potentially destructive initiation; a 'make-or-break' beginning to an enterprise.

Context: In Acts 2.3 the Holy Spirit of God appeared to the believers in Christ on the day of Pentecost as tongues of fire. This is understood as 'baptism in the Spirit' and it prepared the early believers to preach about Jesus; many were later martyred for their faith.

Matthew 3.11 see also Luke 3.16; Acts 2.3
I indeed baptize you with water unto repentance: but he that cometh after me is mightier than I, whose shoes I am not worthy to bear: he shall baptize you with the Holy Ghost, and with fire.

beam / plank in one's own eye

Usage: A reference to the hypocrisy of someone noticing the minor faults of others yet ignoring their own major failings.

Context: One of Jesus' homely images in the Sermon on the Mount, this saying advocates humility and a greater sensitivity to one's own sin than to that of others. Jesus the carpenter would have been very familiar with dust and planks.

Matthew 7.4–5
Or how wilt thou say to thy brother, Let me pull out the mote out of thine eye; and, behold, a beam is in thine own eye? Thou hypocrite, first cast out the beam out of thine own eye; and then shalt thou see clearly to cast out the mote out of thy brother's eye.

bear false witness

Usage: A phrase meaning 'to lie'.

Context: The ninth of the Ten Commandments given by God to Moses for the regulation of his people. Lying, especially in a legal context and against someone who has a call on one's loyalty (one's 'neighbour'), is destructive and abhorrent to God.

> **Exodus 20.16 see also Deuteronomy 5.20**
> *Thou shalt not bear false witness against thy neighbour.*

Behemoth

Usage: Refers to any monstrously big and powerful creature or object; Thomas Hobbes named the Long Parliament as Behemoth in his book *Behemoth*.

Context: Perhaps an elephant or hippopotamus. In the context of Job, God asks Job to consider the animal and marvel at the works of God.

> **Job 40.15**
> *Behold now behemoth, Which I made with thee; He eateth grass as an ox.*

being beside oneself

Usage: Having lost one's grip on reality, especially through rage.

Context: Festus hears Paul's defence of his faith in Christ and concludes he is mad. Paul responds 'I am not mad, but speak forth the words of truth and soberness'.

> **Acts 26.24**
> *And as he thus spake for himself, Festus said with a loud voice, Paul, thou art beside thyself; much learning doth make thee mad.*

bite, or lick, the dust

Usage: Fall to the ground, wounded or dead; used in many cowboy films where the bad guy 'bites the dust'.

Context: In the Bible the term 'lick the dust' is used twice. In Psalm 72 it is used to describe someone who lies postrate before God, so low that they can lick the dust. In Micah 7 the term is used to refer to someone who fears the Lord and comes out of their hole to lick the dust like a serpent.

> **Psalm 72.9 see also Micah 7.17**
> *They that dwell in the wilderness shall bow before him; And his enemies shall lick the dust.*

blind leading the blind

Usage: Refers to bad leaders appointed by people who do not discern their unsuitability for leadership.

Context: In the biblical context Jesus refers to the Pharisees whose teachings prevent the people from responding to God.

> **Matthew 15.14**
> *Let them alone: they be blind leaders of the blind. And if the blind lead the blind, both shall fall into the ditch.*

book of life

Usage: If one's name is in the book of life, one is saved from punishment for sin, safe, or blessed.

Context: The biblical image (frequent in Revelation) refers to the records opened on the Day of Judgement. In a culture where books were valuable and rare the book connotes permanence; the book of life is the record of those saved by Christ.

> **Revelation 3.5**
> *He that overcometh, the same shall be clothed in white raiment; and I will not blot out his name out of the book of life, but I will confess his name before my Father, and before his angels.*

born again

Usage: A term used to describe someone who has a religious conversion to Christianity; also used for people who return to a previous hobby, e.g. born again bikers are motorcyclists who return to motorcycling later in life; the title of a book by Watergate conspirator, Chuck Colson (1976).

Context: Jesus used the term 'born again' in the Bible whilst teaching Nicodemus, a Rabbi of the Jewish sect known as the Pharisees. The traditional Jewish understanding of the promise of salvation was that being rooted in 'the seed of Abraham' referred to physical lineage from Abraham. Jesus explained to Nicodemus that every person must have two births – the natural birth of the physical body, the other of the water and the spirit. This discourse with Nicodemus established the Christian belief that all human beings must be 'born again' of the spiritual seed of Christ. In the Bible, to be 'born again' is associated with terms including new birth, resurrection and new life. Peter also uses the term in one of his letters.

> **John 3.3–7 see also 1 Peter 1.23**
> *Jesus answered and said unto him, Verily, verily, I say unto thee, Except a man be born again, he cannot see the kingdom of God.*

Nicodemus saith unto him, How can a man be born when he is old? can he enter the second time into his mother's womb, and be born? Jesus answered, Verily, verily, I say unto thee, Except a man be born of water and of the Spirit, he cannot enter into the kingdom of God. That which is born of the flesh is flesh; and that which is born of the Spirit is spirit. Marvel not that I said unto thee, Ye must be born again.

born of woman

Usage: Human; mortal and imperfect. 'Not of woman born' is an important phrase in Shakespeare's *Macbeth* and *Of Woman Born* is the title of a book of essays on motherhood by Adrienne Rich.

Context: Humanity is imperfect and fallible. In the New Testament this phrase is echoed in Galatians 4.4 where Paul teaches that Christ's human obedience redeems human nature.

> **Job 14.1 see also Job 15.14; Matthew 11.11**
> *Man that is born of a woman Is of few days, and full of trouble.*

bottomless pit

Usage: A description of an unpleasant situation which cannot be resolved and which swallows up all one's resources.

Context: In the book of Revelation where it occurs frequently this is an image of hell, the place of the Beast.

> **Revelation 9.2**
> *And he opened the bottomless pit; and there arose a smoke out of the pit, as the smoke of a great furnace; and the sun and the air were darkened by reason of the smoke of the pit.*

bowels of compassion

Usage: Deep feeling.

Context: In the age when the King James Bible was translated and published (1611) the emotions were thought of as being seated in the bowels; today they are in the heart. Both imply something deep and powerful.

> **1 John 3.17**
> *But whoso hath this world's good, and seeth his brother have need, and shutteth up his bowels of compassion from him, how dwelleth the love of God in him?*

bread of adversity / affliction

Usage: Trouble and difficulty as an everyday experience.

Context: Isaiah prophesies that although it seems that they are being fed suffering like food, it will not be so forever for God's people. The prophet Micaiah is put in prison for prophesying three bad things about King Ahab. His diet is to be bread and water but the expression seems to imply that more unpleasant things are to accompany it.

> **Isaiah 30.20 see also 1 Kings 22.27**
> *And though the Lord give you the bread of adversity, and the water of affliction, yet shall not thy teachers be removed into a corner any more, but thine eyes shall see thy teachers.*

breathing out threats

Usage: Uttering threats, usually in anger.

Context: Saul (later re-named Paul) takes it upon himself to hound the disciples of Jesus to death; he makes his intentions known.

> **Acts 9.1**
> *And Saul, yet breathing out threatenings and slaughter against the disciples of the Lord, went unto the high priest.*

bringing nothing into the world and carrying nothing out

Usage: The idea is that one ceases to possess anything material when one is dead, just as one came into the world with nothing; one of the opening sentences in the Book of Common Prayer funeral service.

Context: Paul probably echoes Job in this letter: 'Naked came I out of my mother's womb and naked shall I return thither: the LORD gave and the LORD hath taken away; blessed be the name of the LORD' (Job 1.21). Paul makes it an argument for being content with what we have.

> **1 Timothy 6.7**
> *For we brought nothing into this world, and it is certain we can carry nothing out.*

broad way

Usage: Refers to how easy it is to go wrong in life; used in John Bunyan's *Pilgrim's Progress* (1678) for 'Broadway Gate'.

Context: In Jesus' teaching in the Sermon on the Mount this refers to following the crowd instead of standing up for something important because it is difficult. In an age with very few paved roads and little means of transport other than walking, the wide and well-trodden way would be easy to follow.

Matthew 7.13
Enter ye in at the strait gate: for wide is the gate, and broad is the way, that leadeth to destruction, and many there be which go in thereat.

broken reed

Usage: Something that seems to be reliable but proves damaging when trusted.

Context: Papyrus reeds appear strong but are not; when they break they are sharp and dangerous. The image is appropriate both to Egypt (the Nile grows reeds in abundance) and to the disastrous outcome of Israel's reliance on Egypt as an ally.

2 Kings 18.21 see also Isaiah 36.6
Now, behold, thou trustest upon the staff of this bruised reed, even upon Egypt, on which if a man lean, it will go into his hand, and pierce it: so is Pharaoh king of Egypt unto all that trust on him.

bruised reed

Usage: Someone or something damaged and delicate.

Context: This is an image of the love and gentleness of God who treats suffering and damaged people with care: he does not treat people as worthless because they are not strong or brilliant.

Isaiah 42.3 see also Matthew 12.20
A bruised reed shall he not break, and the smoking flax shall he not quench: he shall bring forth judgment unto truth.

burning bush

Usage: A miraculous or startling sign; the burning bush has been used as a symbol by many Reformed Christians starting with the French Huguenots to modern Presbyterians – a symbol of the Church of Scotland.

Context: The fire signifies the presence of God.

Exodus 3.2
And the angel of the LORD appeared unto him in a flame of fire out of the midst of a bush: and he looked, and, behold, the bush burned with fire, and the bush was not consumed.

burying one's talent

Usage: Not using one's gifts.

Context: In this parable Jesus told, some servants used the money ('talent' is a biblical weight, usually of gold or silver) given them by their master, but one buried it in the ground to return it unused when his master came back. He was punished for his neglect.

Matthew 25.25
and I was afraid, and went and hid thy talent in the earth: lo, there thou hast that is thine.

butter someone up

Usage: To flatter or sweet-talk someone.

Context: The contrast between the smooth words and the harsh intention of the speaker is clear in the psalm: his words are deceitful.

Psalm 55.21
The words of his mouth were smoother than butter, but war was in his heart: His words were softer than oil, yet were they drawn swords.

by their fruits ye shall know them

Usage: The outcome of people's actions reveals what kind of people they are.

Context: In Jesus' teaching in the Sermon on the Mount this refers to a means by which the teaching of prophets can be tested: if their words do not come true or evil results from their teaching they are false prophets. By extension, the way Christians live verifies or disproves their profession of faith.

Matthew 7.16–20
Ye shall know them by their fruits. Do men gather grapes of thorns, or figs of thistles? Even so every good tree bringeth forth good fruit; but a corrupt tree bringeth forth evil fruit. A good tree cannot bring forth evil fruit, neither can a corrupt tree bring forth good fruit. Every tree that bringeth not forth good fruit is hewn down, and cast into the fire. Wherefore by their fruits ye shall know them.

cast the first stone

Usage: Be the first to blame someone for something, usually hypocritically.

Context: A woman caught in the act of adultery was brought to Jesus for judgement. The legal penalty for this crime was stoning to death. Jesus teaches that if the law were applied rigidly no one would escape stoning, and he does this by saying that the first stone should be thrown by someone who is sinless. No stone was thrown.

John 8.7
So when they continued asking him, he lifted up himself, and said unto them, He that is without sin among you, let him first cast a stone at her.

cast one's bread upon the waters

Usage: Invest for the future, usually in quiet or kindly ways; not expecting return.

Context: It is unclear what the phrase means precisely. One suggestion is 'to plant seed in waterlogged land'; another is 'to invest in trade by sea'.

> **Ecclesiastes 11.1**
> *Cast thy bread upon the waters: for thou shalt find it after many days.*

casting pearls before swine

Usage: An image of giving something valuable to people who cannot or do not appreciate it.

Context: Jesus used this phrase in the Sermon on the Mount. There is a strong contrast between pearls which are very valuable and pigs who were considered unclean animals by the Jews.

> **Matthew 7.6**
> *Give not that which is holy unto the dogs, neither cast ye your pearls before swine, lest they trample them under their feet, and turn again and rend you.*

chariots of fire

Usage: Often a reference to miraculous speed; the title of a film about Eric Liddell, a record-breaking runner; also a line in William Blake's 'Jerusalem', 'Bring me my chariot of fire'.

Context: The fire, as often in the Bible, signifies the divine. Elijah does not die but is spirited away in the chariot of fire.

> **2 Kings 2.11**
> *And it came to pass, as they still went on, and talked, that, behold, there appeared a chariot of fire, and horses of fire, and parted them both asunder; and Elijah went up by a whirlwind into heaven.*

chasing after the wind

Usage: A pointless exercise or vain hope.

Context: Ecclesiastes explores the meaning of life: the writer concludes that without God, everything is pointless.

> **Ecclesiastes 1.14**
> *I have seen all the works that are done under the sun; and, behold, all is vanity and vexation of spirit.*

chastise with scorpions

Usage: Something turning out much worse than expected.

Context: His people ask the new King Rehoboam for some relief from the burden of labour his father put them under. He decides not to relieve but to increase the burden. A rebellion and the division of the kingdom follows.

> **1 Kings 12.11**
> *And now whereas my father did lade you with a heavy yoke, I will add to your yoke: my father hath chastised you with whips, but I will chastise you with scorpions.*

choose life

Usage: A slogan printed on t-shirts designed by Katharine Hamnett and worn by Wham! in the video for 'Wake Me Up Before You Go Go' and by Roger Taylor in the video for 'Hammer to Fall' (both 1984): the title of a poem by John Hodge which begins the film *Trainspotting* (1996); a pro-life slogan used to encourage women with unplanned/unwanted pregnancies to choose birth over abortion.

Context: In Deuteronomy, God describes how he set before mankind the choice of blessing or cursing, life or death, and encourages man to choose life.

> **Deuteronomy 30.19**
> *I call heaven and earth to record this day against you, that I have set before you life and death, blessing and cursing: therefore choose life, that both thou and thy seed may live.*

clashing cymbal

Usage: Pointless noise or empty words.

Context: In Paul's teaching love is what validates everything in the Church: even inspired speech is worthless without love.

> **1 Corinthians 13.1**
> *Though I speak with the tongues of men and of angels, and have not charity, I am become as sounding brass, or a tinkling cymbal.*

clear as crystal / crystal clear

Usage: Usually in a metaphorical (or often ironic) sense: an idea is well understood and its meaning is obvious; the Crystal Mark is today used by the Plain English Society to denote something that is easy to understand.

Context: Glass was rare in the ancient Near East but naturally occurring crystal was highly valued. Its beauty and clarity as well as its value is appropriate for the heavenly water flowing in the New Jerusalem.

Revelation 22.1
And he shewed me a pure river of water of life, clear as crystal, proceeding out of the throne of God and of the Lamb.

cloud as small as a man's hand

Usage: An apparently insignificant sign heralds a significant or long-awaited change.

Context: After three years of drought in Israel the prophet Elijah prophesied that God would send rain. He sends his servant out seven times to look for the rain and the seventh time he makes this report. The cloud presages the fulfilment of the prophecy.

1 Kings 18.44
And it came to pass at the seventh time, that he said, Behold, there ariseth a little cloud out of the sea, like a man's hand. And he said, Go up, say unto Ahab, Prepare thy chariot, and get thee down, that the rain stop thee not.

cloud of witnesses

Usage: A great crowd or multitude; a vast collection; also used by Christians to mean all the great Christians or saints of the past.

Context: A phrase used to describe those people of faith who have died and are in the presence of Christ in heaven. The Greek word for 'witness' used here is 'martyr'. These, then, are people who have been faithful and whose faith encourages the Christian believer.

Hebrews 12.1
Wherefore seeing we also are compassed about with so great a cloud of witnesses, let us lay aside every weight, and the sin which doth so easily beset us, and let us run with patience the race that is set before us.

coat of many colours

Usage: A woman's riding-coat in former years; a sign of wealth and leisure; popularised in Andrew Lloyd-Webber's musical *Joseph* where it is called the technicolor dreamcoat.

Context: Jacob (Israel) gives his son Joseph a special garment as a sign of special favour; it was naturally galling to his brothers that their brother should be singled out.

Genesis 37.3
Now Israel loved Joseph more than all his children, because he was the son of his old age: and he made him a coat of many colours.

corners of the earth

Usage: From everywhere and anywhere, usually coming together in one place.

Context: In Isaiah, God's people are dispersed over the world but God will gather them into his presence again; in Revelation, the angels guarding the earth hold back destructive winds from the outer parts, the four corners of the earth.

> **Isaiah 11.12 see also Revelation 7.1**
> *And he shall set up an ensign for the nations, and shall assemble the outcasts of Israel, and gather together the dispersed of Judah from the four corners of the earth.*

cornerstone

Usage: The fundamental basis of an argument on which the rest is built; of a person, the one around whom a team is built.

Context: This is an important image in the early Christian understanding of who Jesus was: it showed from the Old Testament scripture that Jesus would be rejected even though he was the very foundation of God's building. There is some interchange in textual and translation history between 'cornerstone' and 'capstone', which have different architectural purposes.

> **Psalm 118.22 see also Matthew 21.42**
> *The stone which the builders refused Is become the head stone of the corner.*

counting the cost

Usage: Usually metaphorically applied: facing up to the long-term demands of any enterprise.

Context: In Jesus' teaching this is one of several illustrations of the necessary thought and calculation that has to be given to the commitment of following him.

> **Luke 14.28**
> *For which of you, intending to build a tower, sitteth not down first, and counteth the cost, whether he have sufficient to finish it?*

crown of thorns

Usage: Sometimes used of an unmerited affliction.

Context: Jesus was crowned in mockery: the charge-sheet on his cross was 'King of the Jews' and this was his crown.

> **Matthew 27.29**
> *And when they had platted a crown of thorns, they put it upon his head, and a reed in his right hand:*

*and they bowed the knee before him, and mocked
him, saying, Hail, King of the Jews!*

cup runneth over

Usage: Usually expressing the contentment of
unexpectedly having more than enough of something;
sometimes used ironically.

Context: The imagery of feasting with abundance
of food and drink expresses the psalmist's joy in
the presence of God.

> **Psalm 23.5**
> *Thou preparest a table before me in the presence
> of mine enemies: Thou anointest my head with
> oil; my cup runneth over.*

daily bread

Usage: The necessities of life.

Context: From the Lord's Prayer, a pattern of prayer
for Christians which includes a petition for daily
needs of food and forgiveness.

> **Matthew 6.11**
> *Give us this day our daily bread.*

Damascus road

Usage: A sudden transformation or enlightenment
which changes a person.

Context: Saul is on his way to Damascus to imprison
and punish Christians, but is struck blind by a light
and hears the voice of Christ. He changes dramatically
to become the most effective preacher of Christ,
a transformation signalled by his change of name
to Paul.

> **Acts 9.3**
> *And as he journeyed, he came near Damascus:
> and suddenly there shined round about him a
> light from heaven.*

darkness that can be felt

Usage: Darkness that has an oppressive or unnatural
aspect.

Context: This was one of the plagues inflicted on
the Egyptians because Pharaoh would not let the
people of Israel go free from slavery. It was an
unnatural total darkness for three days.

> **Exodus 10.21**
> *And the LORD said unto Moses, Stretch out thine
> hand toward heaven, that there may be darkness
> over the land of Egypt, even darkness which may
> be felt.*

David and Goliath

Usage: A pair of disputants or combatants of disproportionate size or ability.

Context: David the shepherd-boy hears Goliath the very tall Philistine challenging the armies of Israel. David kills Goliath with a stone from his sling.

> **1 Samuel 17.4 see also 1 Samuel 17.23**
> *And there went out a champion out of the camp of the Philistines, named Goliath, of Gath, whose height was six cubits and a span.*

day of judgement

Usage: Refers to a decisive assessment or turning-point in a project or someone getting their come-uppance.

Context: In the Old Testament the term 'the day of the Lord' is used for this concept. Throughout the Bible there is the conviction that God will judge people and that this will happen at a particular but unknown time.

> **Matthew 10.15**
> *Verily I say unto you, It shall be more tolerable for the land of Sodom and Gomorrha in the day of judgment, than for that city.*

deep calls to deep

Usage: Usually an image of unspoken understanding between two people.

Context: In the biblical context the writer is overwhelmed with sorrow pressing him down like the weight of water in a waterfall.

> **Psalm 42.7**
> *Deep calleth unto deep at the noise of thy waterspouts: All thy waves and thy billows are gone over me.*

den of thieves / robbers

Usage: A reference to a gathering of people who seem like crooks.

Context: Jesus expels the traders from the Temple area in Jerusalem ('the house of prayer', so called in Isaiah 56.7). The Temple is the place where God is specially present. However, the traders have made the worship of pilgrims a profitable business.

> **Matthew 21.13**
> *and said unto them, It is written, My house shall be called the house of prayer; but ye have made it a den of thieves.*

digging a hole for oneself

Usage: Contriving a scheme to discomfit someone else but becoming the victim of it oneself.

Context: In a literal sense, pits were used to trap animals; in a metaphorical sense, this phrase refers to any scheming against another that backfires on the schemer.

> **Proverbs 26.27 see also Ecclesiastes 10.8; Psalm 57.6**
> *Whoso diggeth a pit shall fall therein: And he that rolleth a stone, it will return upon him.*

do not muzzle the ox

Usage: Do not deny a person/animal legitimate reward or some benefit from their labour to someone.

Context: Paul writes to Timothy following this quote from Deuteronomy 25.4: 'Thou shalt not muzzle the ox when he treadeth out the corn.' Oxen were used in the threshing and grinding of corn and to muzzle them would be to stop them eating any of it during the process. The biblical idea is that it is fair and reasonable for the ox to be able to enjoy the benefit of eating during its work.

> **1 Timothy 5.18**
> *For the scripture saith, Thou shalt not muzzle the ox that treadeth out the corn. And, The labourer is worthy of his reward.*

dog returning to its vomit

Usage: A reference to someone returning to bad habits or wickedness of any sort.

Context: In Proverbs the fool is the one who does not learn from his mistakes. In Peter the proverb refers to those who once were apparently Christians but who turned from the faith back into sin.

> **Proverbs 26.11 see also 2 Peter 2.22**
> *As a dog returneth to his vomit, So a fool returneth to his folly.*

doing what is right in one's own eyes

Usage: May describe someone pursuing a selfish course of action; or following one's own conscience based on conflicting choices.

Context: In the book of Judges this saying occurs frequently, referring to the near-anarchy of the time; it recognises the good intentions of the people but indicates that they were in rebellion with God. The Proverbs passage refers to the unfounded self-confidence of the fool.

Judges 17.6 see also Proverbs 12.15
In those days there was no king in Israel, but every man did that which was right in his own eyes.

don't let the sun go down on your anger

Usage: Advice to not give resentment a chance to grow.

Context: Paul advises to resolve disputes within a limited time like a day.

Ephesians 4.26
Be ye angry, and sin not: let not the sun go down upon your wrath.

doubting Thomas

Usage: A term that is used to describe a sceptic, or someone who will refuse to believe something without direct, physical, personal evidence.

Context: The term is based on the story of Thomas the Apostle, a disciple of Jesus who doubted Jesus' resurrection and demanded to feel Jesus' wounds before being convinced. After seeing Jesus alive and being offered the opportunity to touch his wounds, Thomas then professed his faith in Jesus. The biblical account then reports that Jesus said, 'Blessed are they that have not seen, and yet have believed', suggesting that Jesus' preference was for faith over scepticism.

John 20.24–29
But Thomas, one of the twelve, called Didymus, was not with them when Jesus came. The other disciples therefore said unto him, We have seen the Lord. But he said unto them, Except I shall see in his hands the print of the nails, and put my finger into the print of the nails, and thrust my hand into his side, I will not believe.
And after eight days again his disciples were within, and Thomas with them: then came Jesus, the doors being shut, and stood in the midst, and said, Peace be unto you. Then saith he to Thomas, Reach hither thy finger, and behold my hands; and reach hither thy hand, and thrust it into my side: and be not faithless, but believing. And Thomas answered and said unto him, My Lord and my God. Jesus saith unto him, Thomas, because thou hast seen me, thou hast believed: blessed are they that have not seen, and yet have believed.

driving like Jehu

Usage: A witty borrowing of the idea of driving, transferred from driving horses harnessed to a chariot to driving a motor vehicle.

Context: Jehu was a famously fierce soldier whose chariot-driving followed his temperament.

> **2 Kings 9.20**
> *And the watchman told, saying, He came even unto them, and cometh not again: and the driving is like the driving of Jehu the son of Nimshi; for he driveth furiously.*

drop in a bucket / drop in the ocean

Usage: A tiny insignificant amount.

Context: The Bible often uses images of size to represent importance: here the writer emphasises that God did not consult with or exert himself in creating all the nations he created.

> **Isaiah 40.15**
> *Behold, the nations are as a drop of a bucket, and are counted as the small dust of the balance: behold, he taketh up the isles as a very little thing.*

dry bones

Usage: Refers to the outline or skeleton of an idea which must be 'fleshed out'; a well-known Negro spiritual song.

Context: Ezekiel's vision is of God's power to resurrect the dead bones and give them life: in the same way, Ezekiel is to prophesy to God's despairing people that they will live in their own land, bringing life to their dead hopes.

> **Ezekiel 37.1–2**
> *The hand of the LORD was upon me, and carried me out in the spirit of the LORD, and set me down in the midst of the valley which was full of bones, and caused me to pass by them round about: and, behold, there were very many in the open valley; and, lo, they were very dry.*

dust to dust

Usage: A phrase used in funeral services indicating that physical bodies will decay back into the elements from which they were first composed.

Context: In the biblical idea, humanity has a physical component which is earthly ('dust') and a spiritual component (breath or spirit). At death the dust returns to the earth.

> **Genesis 3.19**
> *in the sweat of thy face shalt thou eat bread, till thou return unto the ground; for out of it wast thou taken: for dust thou art, and unto dust shalt thou return.*

ears to hear

Usage: A phrase referring to someone who intentionally listens, desiring to fully understand what is being said to them.

Context: The phrase in the Bible, repeated frequently, highlights the fact that it is possible to hear without understanding or obeying.

> **Matthew 11.15**
> *He that hath ears to hear, let him hear.*

East of Eden

Usage: The title of a novel by John Steinbeck (1952; a film followed in 1955); possibly a reference to a decline of fortunes (the novel deals with the experience of people being driven from their homes).

Context: After killing his brother, Cain was banished from his home to wander east of Eden.

> **Genesis 4.16**
> *And Cain went out from the presence of the LORD, and dwelt in the land of Nod, on the east of Eden.*

eat, drink and be merry

Usage: Refers to thoughtless unreflective pleasure; occurs many times in modern English-language popular culture where it is also associated with the Latin phrase *carpe diem* meaning 'seize the day'. The Bible uses this phrase variously.

Context:
- 'Eat and drink for tomorrow we die' derives from verses in Isaiah 22.13 and 1 Corinthians 15.32, both in a negative context illustrating a life without faith.
- the man is a fool (Luke 12) who ignores the fact that he will die without having made provision for his soul.
- in Ecclesiastes pleasure is seen as a positive principle in human life, as indeed it is in, passage where a celebration is being organised for the returning prodigal son (Luke 15).

> **Isaiah 22.13 see also 1 Corinthians 15.32;**
> **Luke 12.19; Luke 15.23; Ecclesiastes 8.15**
> *and behold joy and gladness, slaying oxen, and killing sheep, eating flesh, and drinking wine: let us eat and drink; for to morrow we shall die.*

entertaining angels unawares

Usage: The idea that kindness may have a significance out of proportion to its apparent impact.

Context: In the Old Testament angels sometimes represent God; in the New Testament Jesus teaches that when kindness is done to others it is done for him (Matthew 25). Hebrews inherits this tradition:

as Paul writes, 'Let brotherly love continue. Be not forgetful to entertain strangers: for thereby some have entertained angels unawares.'

Genesis 18.2 see also Genesis 18.16, 19.1; Hebrews 13.1–2
and he lift up his eyes and looked, and, lo, three men stood by him: and when he saw them, he ran to meet them from the tent door, and bowed himself toward the ground.

evil eye

Usage: The superstition that the way someone looks at you may have a malign power.

Context: In the Bible passages the eye represents the interpretative faculty, the way we see things both literally and in terms of understanding. If we are mean then we watch how much people eat (Proverbs); and if we are wicked we see everything in a distorted unpleasant way (Matthew).

Proverbs 23.6; Matthew 6.23
Eat thou not the bread of him that hath an evil eye, Neither desire thou his dainty meats.

eye of a needle

Usage: An image of impossibility.

Context: Refers to the impossibility of passing a camel through the eye of a needle; a metaphor originally used by Jesus for how difficult it is for a person of wealth to enter the kingdom of God.

Matthew 19.24
And again I say unto you, It is easier for a camel to go through the eye of a needle, than for a rich man to enter into the kingdom of God.

eye for an eye

Usage: The idea that a person pays back a wrong done to them with a similar wrong.

Context: This rule (known as the *lex talionis*) provided for a precise correspondence between the penalty and the injury caused: if one knocked out someone's tooth then the law required that the one who knocked out the tooth should also have a tooth knocked out. Its rigid fairness was designed to limit retribution so that it was fair, and not greater than that received. Jesus significantly modified this by emphasising the need to 'go the extra mile'.

Exodus 21.24 see also Deuteronomy 19.21; Matthew 5.38–42
eye for eye, tooth for tooth, hand for hand, foot for foot, burning for burning, wound for wound, stripe for stripe.

eyes to the blind

Usage: A byword for someone who clarifies something.

Context: Job protests his innocence of wrongdoing against those who claim that his suffering is deserved and gives many instances of his good deeds – among them, helping the blind and lame.

> **Job 29.15**
> *I was eyes to the blind, And feet was I to the lame.*

faith to move mountains

Usage: A person's faith can overcome every obstacle in their way.

Context: Jesus often uses physical images to teach about spiritual things. Faith can change things that loom as large as mountains.

> **Matthew 21.21**
> *Jesus answered and said unto them, Verily I say unto you, If ye have faith, and doubt not, ye shall not only do this which is done to the fig tree, but also if ye shall say unto this mountain, Be thou removed, and be thou cast into the sea; it shall be done.*

faith, hope and charity

Usage: The three greatest Christian values. Charity is often called love.

Context: In Christian tradition these are the three theological virtues, the core values of the faith.

> **1 Corinthians 13.13**
> *And now abideth faith, hope, charity, these three; but the greatest of these is charity.*

fall flat on his face

Usage: Describes failing completely in front of others, often in an embarrassing way, at something a person has set out to do.

Context: The Bible reflects the custom, still evident in the Middle East, that people used to bow prostrate in front of people in higher authority, or in prayer. This was called falling flat on your face and is used throughout the Bible.

> **Genesis 17.3 see also Numbers 22.31**
> *And Abram fell on his face: and God talked with him.*

fall from grace

Usage: Most often this refers to the failure of someone who had promised great things.

Context: Paul's argument is over the effectiveness of good deeds as against God's unmerited mercy. He says that if one trusts in good deeds, grace becomes unnecessary – but no one can be good enough. Only God's grace will save a person.

Galatians 5.4
Christ is become of no effect unto you, whosoever of you are justified by the law; ye are fallen from grace.

falling by the wayside

Usage: Dropping out of some project either accidentally or because it is difficult.

Context: In Jesus' parable of the sower, the seed represents the gospel which is preached to everyone just as the sower throws out his seed on the ground. Only some seed grows and produces a crop. Some falls onto pathways and is eaten by the birds, which is here an image of those who take no heed of the message.

Matthew 13.4
and when he sowed, some seeds fell by the way side, and the fowls came and devoured them up.

false prophet

Usage: One whose predictions turn out to be wrong.

Context: In the Bible false prophets are those who teach untrue things about God, those who report as God's words their own false ideas and those who make false predictions about the future.

Matthew 24.11
And many false prophets shall rise, and shall deceive many.

fat of the land

Usage: All kinds of good things, usually for eating and drinking.

Context: Pharaoh promised Joseph's family, who had originally come to Egypt to buy food in a time of famine, that they will have the best that Egypt can offer. The phrase may also be influenced by the fat cows of Pharoah's dreams, which indicated plenty. Fat is generally a positive thing in the Bible.

Genesis 45.18
and take your father and your households, and come unto me: and I will give you the good of the land of Egypt, and ye shall eat the fat of the land.

fatted calf

Usage: A special gift or meal.

Context: The fatted calf was a specially fed animal destined for a feast. Here the feast is to welcome home the prodigal son.

> **Luke 15.23**
> *and bring hither the fatted calf, and kill it; and let us eat, and be merry.*

fear of the Lord is the beginning of wisdom

Usage: For someone to be wise they need to start by humbly respecting the guidance given by God; 'fear of God' is also used as a threatening term, e.g 'putting the fear of God' into someone.

Context: Wisdom is not a mere intellectual or social gift: it is essentially about knowing and acknowledging God ('fear' means respect as well as fear).

> **Psalm 111.10 see also Proverbs 1.7; Proverbs 9.10**
> *The fear of the LORD is the beginning of wisdom.*

feeding of the 5,000

Usage: A meal for a large number, usually when there might not be quite enough food.

Context: Jesus uses the faith of his disciples and a boy to feed a large crowd with five bread loaves and two fish.

> **Matthew 14.21**
> *And they that had eaten were about five thousand men, beside women and children.*

feet of clay

Usage: The discovery that someone impressive has ordinary human failings.

Context: This image is seen in a vision by King Nebuchadnezzar. In the vision a rock smashes the clay feet of a statue made from gold, silver, brass and iron, and thus the whole thing is brought down because of the weakness of the clay feet.

> **Daniel 2.33**
> *his legs of iron, his feet part of iron and part of clay.*

fiery furnace

Usage: A horrible place to be thrown into as punishment for disobedience.

Context: The furnace is devised as a torture for those who disobey the king's command to worship an idol. Three friends do disobey but are saved in the furnace by the presence of a divine figure.

> **Daniel 3.6**
> *and whoso falleth not down and worshippeth shall the same hour be cast into the midst of a burning fiery furnace.*

fight the good fight

Usage: Work hard for a worthy cause; also a well-known hymn by John Monsell.

Context: In the Bible the Christian life is sometimes seen in military terms.

> **1 Timothy 6.12**
> *Fight the good fight of faith, lay hold on eternal life, whereunto thou art also called, and hast professed a good profession before many witnesses.*

figs from thistles

Usage: Refers to an impossible outcome.

Context: In Jesus' teaching in the Sermon on the Mount this refers to a means by which the teaching of prophets can be tested. The impossibility of gathering figs from thistles represents the impossibility of good results from false prophecy.

> **Matthew 7.16**
> *Ye shall know them by their fruits. Do men gather grapes of thorns, or figs of thistles?*

fire and brimstone

Usage: Preaching that makes frequent reference to hell and its torments.

Context: John's vision of judgement paints hell in the lurid colours and smells of volcanic eruption. Brimstone is sulphur which burns slowly with an acrid smell.

> **Revelation 14.10**
> *the same shall drink of the wine of the wrath of God, which is poured out without mixture into the cup of his indignation; and he shall be tormented with fire and brimstone in the presence of the holy angels, and in the presence of the Lamb.*

first shall be last and the last shall be first

Usage: An acknowledgement that a person's estimation of their own importance may be very overrated and vice versa.

Context: Jesus teaches that status from a human perspective is worthless; his evaluation is more important and is eternal.

Matthew 19.30
*But many that are first shall be last; and the last
shall be first.*

five loaves and two fishes

Usage: A small amount needing to be distributed
among many.

Context: Jesus uses the faith of his disciples and
a boy to feed a large crowd with five loaves of bread
and two fish.

Matthew 14.17
*And they say unto him, We have here but five
loaves, and two fishes.*

fixing (setting) one's heart on something

Usage: Keeping something as the fundamental desire
and inclination.

Context: The Israelites and Christians are urged
to find stability by making the service and love of
God their desire.

1 Chronicles 22.19 see also Psalm 57.7
*Now set your heart and your soul to seek the
LORD your God; arise therefore, and build ye the
sanctuary of the LORD God, to bring the ark of
the covenant of the LORD, and the holy vessels
of God, into the house that is to be built to the
name of the LORD.*

flesh and blood

Usage: One's 'flesh and blood' is used to refer to
one's family; also used to denote the living material
of which people are composed.

Context: The term appears a number of times in the
New Testament, when it is used to mean humankind.
Jesus said to Simon Peter 'Blessed art thou, Simon
Barjona: for flesh and blood hath not revealed it
unto thee, but my Father which is in heaven.'

Matthew 16.17 see also Ephesians 6.12
*And Jesus answered and said unto him, Blessed
art thou, Simon Bar-jona: for flesh and blood hath
not revealed it unto thee, but my Father which
is in heaven.*

fleshpots

Usage: Usually refers to any physical (often sexual)
pleasure that is illicit and the place where such
pleasure may be found.

Context: The flesh pots were vessels for cooking
meat; the Israelites hanker after meat in their
desert wanderings and remember this aspect of life

in Egypt rather than the fact that God had saved them from slavery.

Exodus 16.3
and the children of Israel said unto them, Would to God we had died by the hand of the LORD in the land of Egypt, when we sat by the flesh pots, and when we did eat bread to the full; for ye have brought us forth into this wilderness, to kill this whole assembly with hunger.

fly in the ointment

Usage: Something that spoils an otherwise good thing.

Context: Even a tiny impurity like a dead fly can spoil a costly perfume, in the same way a small misjudgement can ruin the reputation of a wise man.

Ecclesiastes 10.1
Dead flies cause the ointment of the apothecary to send forth a stinking savour: so doth a little folly him that is in reputation for wisdom and honour.

fool and his money are soon parted

Usage: Stupid people spend their money as fast as they get it.

Context: Wisdom includes practical prudence with regard to money; a fool is profligate.

Proverbs 21.20
There is treasure to be desired and oil in the dwelling of the wise; But a foolish man spendeth it up.

for / to everything a season

Usage: There is a proper time for everything to be done or said; this is often used to suggest that something recently done or said was not at the right time. 'Turn! Turn! Turn! (to Everything There is a Season)' was a well known song by Peter Seeger.

Context: The biblical context refers to the interlocking movements of history in the individual's life and the nation's: birth and death, war and peace. All of these lie in the power of God.

Ecclesiastes 3.1
To every thing there is a season, and a time to every purpose under the heaven.

forbidden fruit

Usage: Something which is prohibited or forbidden.

Context: The term originates from the story of the Garden of Eden. In the story God forbade Adam and Eve to touch the fruit of the tree of knowledge.

Genesis 2.9–17
And out of the ground made the LORD God to grow every tree that is pleasant to the sight, and good for food; the tree of life also in the midst of the garden, and the tree of knowledge of good and evil. And a river went out of Eden to water the garden; and from thence it was parted, and became into four heads. The name of the first is Pison: that is it which compasseth the whole land of Havilah, where there is gold; and the gold of that land is good: there is bdellium and the onyx stone. And the name of the second river is Gihon: the same is it that compasseth the whole land of Ethiopia. And the name of the third river is Hiddekel: that is it which goeth toward the east of Assyria. And the fourth river is Euphrates. And the LORD God took the man, and put him into the garden of Eden to dress it and to keep it. And the LORD God commanded the man, saying, Of every tree of the garden thou mayest freely eat: but of the tree of the knowledge of good and evil, thou shalt not eat of it: for in the day that thou eatest thereof thou shalt surely die.

found wanting

Usage: Failing to meet expectations.

Context: 'Wanting' means 'lacking': here, lacking in everything God approves. At Belshazzar's feast a mysterious finger writes on the wall what amounts to a judgement on the king.

Daniel 5.27
Thou art weighed in the balances, and art found wanting.

four horsemen of the apocalypse

Usage: A series of terrible events that seem too much to bear.

Context: The four horses and horsemen represent (approximately) conquest, discord, judgement and death; waves of events that assault the people in the last days of earth when the Bible says that God will decisively defeat the forces of evil.

Revelation 6.8
And I looked, and behold a pale horse: and his name that sat on him was Death, and Hell followed with him. And power was given unto them over the fourth part of the earth, to kill with sword, and with hunger, and with death, and with the beasts of the earth.

foursquare

Usage: Solid, reliable.

Context: John's vision of the New Jerusalem, the City of God. Literally interpreted, the city is square but the reference is equally to the quality of solidity and unshakableness.

> **Revelation 21.16**
> *And the city lieth foursquare, and the length is as large as the breadth: and he measured the city with the reed, twelve thousand furlongs. The length and the breadth and the height of it are equal.*

from strength to strength

Usage: Continual improvement, or progress from one success to another higher level of success; often refers to someone recovering from a serious illness.

Context: The term was a Hebrew idiom used in a psalm, where the psalmist refers to someone whose strength in the Lord increases daily.

> **Psalm 84.7**
> *They go from strength to strength, Every one of them in Zion appeareth before God.*

gadarene swine

Usage: Man, with his ability to sin, has been filled with evil and become like that herd of maddened swine racing towards his own destruction.

Context: In all exorcisms except one Jesus simply expelled the demons. But at Gadara (or Gerasa or Gergesa) Jesus sent the demons into a herd of pigs.

> **Luke 8.33–34**
> *Then went the devils out of the man, and entered into the swine: and the herd ran violently down a steep place into the lake, and were choked. When they that fed them saw what was done, they fled, and went and told it in the city and in the country.*

generation of vipers (sometimes also 'brood of vipers')

Usage: A disparaging reference to a group of people who are potentially dangerous to the speaker.

Context: John the Baptist forthrightly attributes both cunning and potential evil intent to the religious leaders of his day.

> **Matthew 3.7**
> *But when he saw many of the Pharisees and Sadducees come to his baptism, he said unto them, O generation of vipers, who hath warned you to flee from the wrath to come?*

get thee behind me Satan

Usage: A demand that anyone suggesting an alternative to the one proposed by the speaker should give way.

Context: In the New Testament, Satan is the evil enemy of God who seeks to deflect Jesus from his mission and is reprimanded by Jesus.

> Luke 4.8
> *And Jesus answered and said unto him, Get thee behind me, Satan: for it is written, Thou shalt worship the Lord thy God, and him only shalt thou serve.*

girding one's loins

Usage: Getting ready for something that will require a lot of effort.

Context: Very frequently used in the Bible, both of physical and spiritual effort; this phrase refers to gathering up long robes to free the legs.

> 1 Kings 18.46 see also Job 38.3; Job 40.7;
> 1 Peter 1.13
> *And the hand of the LORD was on Elijah; and he girded up his loins, and ran before Ahab to the entrance of Jezreel.*

giving up the ghost

Usage: To die or abandon hope.

Context: In the biblical idea humanity has a physical component which is earthly ('dust') and a spiritual component (breath, spirit or as here 'ghost'). When we die the spirit or ghost departs or returns to God.

> Mark 15.37
> *And Jesus cried with a loud voice, and gave up the ghost.*

gnashing of teeth

Usage: Loud expressions of complaint, regret or remorse.

Context: Those in torment grind their teeth in agony.

> Matthew 25.30
> *And cast ye the unprofitable servant into outer darkness: there shall be weeping and gnashing of teeth.*

go forth and multiply

Usage: Associated with marriages producing children; in modern usage, also a swear phrase to tell someone to go away.

Context: God's blessing or command. After creating the animals 'God blessed them, saying, Be fruitful,

and multiply, and fill the waters in the seas, and
let fowl multiply in the earth.'

Genesis 1.22
*And God blessed them, saying, Be fruitful, and
multiply, and fill the waters in the seas, and let
fowl multiply in the earth.*

go the extra mile

Usage: Do more than is strictly required.

Context: A Roman soldier could require any citizen to
carry a burden for a mile; Jesus says that a Christian
should do more for the sake of love, even for those
who were widely hated and feared.

Matthew 5.41
*And whosoever shall compel thee to go a mile, go
with him twain.*

go to (consider) the ant you sluggard

Usage: A recommendation to be active.

Context: Ants have strength and persistence out
of proportion to their size from which we can
learn lessons.

Proverbs 6.6
*Go to the ant, thou sluggard; Consider her ways,
and be wise.*

God forbid

Usage: An imprecation expressing a wish that
something may not happen or be the case.

Context: In origin a prayer that God may prevent the
undesirable event or situation but often used in the
Bible to imply that a suggested action is contrary
to (forbidden by) God's will.

Genesis 44.7
*And they said unto him, Wherefore saith my lord
these words? God forbid that thy servants should
do according to this thing.*

God is not mocked

Usage: Refers to the notion that events never turn
out contrary to God's will.

Context: Paul teaches that humans can never have
the upper hand against God; God will make justice
prevail.

Galatians 6.7
*Be not deceived; God is not mocked: for whatsoever
a man soweth, that shall he also reap.*

God loves a cheerful giver

Usage: Be generous.

Context: Paul requests gifts from the church at Corinth for the relief of suffering but he asks that people do it gladly in response to God's love, not out of duty.

> **2 Corinthians 9.7**
> *Every man according as he purposeth in his heart, so let him give; not grudgingly, or of necessity: for God loveth a cheerful giver.*

God save the King / Queen

Usage: Popular cry in favour of the reigning monarch, also proclaimed during the coronation ceremony; the national anthem of the United Kingdom.

Context: Samuel has anointed Saul king and now proclaims him to the people; the people respond with the acclamation suggesting that the appointment is God's.

> **1 Samuel 10.24**
> *And Samuel said to all the people, See ye him whom the LORD hath chosen, that there is none like him among all the people? And all the people shouted, and said, God save the king.*

going from strength to strength

Usage: Getting better and better at something.

Context: The psalm refers to those who undertake the arduous trip to Jerusalem to worship God. The sight of the Temple in the distance gives them especial vigour because they can see their destination and all that it means.

> **Psalm 84.7**
> *They go from strength to strength, Every one of them in Zion appeareth before God.*

golden calf

Usage: An idol.

Context: In the temporary absence of Moses, Aaron gives in to the people's wish for a tangible 'god' to worship. The people were returning to a golden calf which was an Egyptian god.

> **Exodus 32.2-4 see also 2 Kings 10.29;**
> **2 Chronicles 13.8**
> *And Aaron said unto them, Break off the golden earrings, which are in the ears of your wives, of your sons, and of your daughters, and bring them unto me. And all the people brake off the golden earrings which were in their ears, and brought them unto Aaron. And he received them at their hand, and fashioned it with a graving tool, after*

*he had made it a molten calf: and they said, These
be thy gods, O Israel, which brought thee up out
of the land of Egypt.*

good Samaritan

Usage: Someone who is unexpectedly caring and
generous; the Samaritans is a charity which provides
emotional support to anyone in distress, most often
via its telephone helpline.

Context: Jesus' parable answers the question, 'Who is
my neighbour?' A Jewish man who has been attacked
and robbed is helped by a Samaritan. In normal
circumstances these two people groups despised
each other, but the Samaritan takes responsibility
for the injured man and acts as his neighbour. Jesus
thus challenges his hearers' assumptions and explains
the true meaning of neighbour.

> **Luke 10.33**
> *But a certain Samaritan, as he journeyed, came
> where he was: and when he saw him, he had
> compassion on him.*

good shepherd

Usage: Faithful and honourable leader of people.

Context: The Bible often uses the image of shepherd
and sheep to refer to the relationship between God
and his people. Here Jesus is the good shepherd who
protects and dies for his sheep.

> **John 10.11**
> *I am the good shepherd: the good shepherd giveth
> his life for the sheep.*

grain of mustard / mustard seed

Usage: Refers to a disproportionate relation between
something and the effect it might have.

Context: Jesus proposes the difficult idea that even
the tiniest faith in God can have momentous effects.

> **Matthew 17.20**
> *And Jesus said unto them, Because of your unbelief:
> for verily I say unto you, If ye have faith as a grain
> of mustard seed, ye shall say unto this mountain,
> Remove hence to yonder place; and it shall remove;
> and nothing shall be impossible unto you.*

grapes of wrath

Usage: An image of vengeance, possibly depending
on the redness of the grape-juice and the process of
crushing they undergo to produce wine; the title of
a novel by John Steinbeck (1939); mentioned in the
Battle Hymn of the Republic (1861), 'he is trampling out
the vintage where the grapes of wrath are stored'.

Context: The Bible uses many reaping and harvesting images to refer to the Last Judgement, as here.

> **Revelation 14.19**
> *And the angel thrust in his sickle into the earth, and gathered the vine of the earth, and cast it into the great winepress of the wrath of God.*

great men are not always wise

Usage: Power doesn't equal wisdom.

Context: The wisdom literature of the Old Testament explores the relationships between prosperity and suffering, success and justice among others. Here Elihu is arguing that age, success and the large number of people who might agree with you does not necessarily mean you are right.

> **Job 32.9**
> *Great men are not always wise: Neither do the aged understand judgment.*

greater love hath no man

Usage: A reference usually to someone who has sacrificed themselves for others; often found on gravestones and memorials.

Context: Jesus implies that since his disciples are his friends he is willing to die for them. They in turn died for him and the Church.

> **John 15.13**
> *Greater love hath no man than this, that a man lay down his life for his friends.*

grey hair is a glorious crown

Usage: Old age is a good thing.

Context: Old people were respected as wise and important in early societies, and grey hair is a characteristic of age.

> **Proverbs 16.31**
> *The hoary head is a crown of glory, If it be found in the way of righteousness.*

harvest festival

Usage: A celebration of the autumn harvest; in the United Kingdom, many churches, especially in villages, often include a harvest supper, which is a meal made from local produce; in North America early English colonists continued this tradition where it is today known as Thanksgiving.

Context: Three harvest festivals are mandated in the Bible. There was a seven-day springtime festival of Unleavened Bread, around the barley harvest; an early summer harvest festival, when the wheat ripens; and an autumnal festival of Ingathering, when olives, grapes and other fruits were harvested.

Exodus 23.14–17
Three times thou shalt keep a feast unto me in the year. Thou shalt keep the feast of unleavened bread: (thou shalt eat unleavened bread seven days, as I commanded thee, in the time appointed of the month Abib; for in it thou camest out from Egypt: and none shall appear before me empty:) and the feast of harvest, the firstfruits of thy labours, which thou hast sown in the field: and the feast of ingathering, which is in the end of the year, when thou hast gathered in thy labours out of the field. Three times in the year all thy males shall appear before the Lord GOD.

haves and have-nots

Usage: To those who are materially well-off (the haves) and those who are not (the have-nots).

Context: Jesus is essentially referring to spiritual understanding rather than material possessions.

Matthew 13.12
For whosoever hath, to him shall be given, and he shall have more abundance: but whosoever hath not, from him shall be taken away even that he hath.

having a cross to bear

Usage: Usually refers to a chronic problem or difficulty that dogs an individual.

Context: Criminals carried their cross to the place of execution. Jesus is making the point that following him may involve being the butt of the contempt and extreme spite of others. The phrase may also have been influenced by the story of Simon of Cyrene being made to carry the cross of Jesus.

Matthew 10.38 see also Matthew 16.24
And he that taketh not his cross, and followeth after me, is not worthy of me.

head on a plate

Usage: To sacrifice someone's position or career in reparation for a disastrous policy or plan.

Context: Known to tradition as Salome, the girl persuades King Herod to have John the Baptist killed. John had criticised Herod for marrying his brother's wife Herodias, Salome's mother.

Matthew 14.8
And she, being before instructed of her mother, said, Give me here John Baptist's head in a charger.

heap burning coals on someone's head

Usage: Doing a good deed to someone who hates us and thus shaming the beneficiary of the deed.

Context: The burning coals are a metaphor for the deep embarrassment that someone might feel if someone they hate helps them when they need it.

> **Proverbs 25.21–22 see also Romans 12.20**
> *If thine enemy be hungry, give him bread to eat; And if he be thirsty, give him water to drink: For thou shalt heap coals of fire upon his head, And the LORD shall reward thee.*

heart of stone

Usage: Unfeeling, without proper human responses.

Context: Ezekiel refers to the time when God will gather his people together and give them a responsive and loving spirit in the place of their indifference to him.

> **Ezekiel 11.19**
> *And I will give them one heart, and I will put a new spirit within you; and I will take the stony heart out of their flesh, and will give them an heart of flesh:*

hip and thigh

Usage: To inflict vicious defeat and damage upon someone.

Context: Samson takes revenge on the Philistines, killing many 'with a great slaughter'.

> **Judges 15.8**
> *And he smote them hip and thigh with a great slaughter: and he went down and dwelt in the top of the rock Etam.*

hollow of one's hand

Usage: Having control of a situation; the concave bowl made by the cupped hand.

Context: As often the Bible images the world as minute compared to God its creator. Having the world in his palm moreover suggests that God holds and tends his creation.

> **Isaiah 40.12**
> *Who hath measured the waters in the hollow of his hand, and meted out heaven with the span, and comprehended the dust of the earth in a measure, and weighed the mountains in scales, and the hills in a balance?*

honeyed words

Usage: Persuasive, possibly flattering words.

Context: Pleasant words can be true or false, deceiving or affirming. The prostitute's words lure the unwary but pleasant words honestly spoken make for peace and harmony.

> Proverbs 5.3 see also Proverbs 16.24
> *For the lips of a strange woman drop as an honeycomb, And her mouth is smoother than oil.*

hope deferred makes the heart sick

Usage: When one's hopes are not fulfilled one tends to feel let down and despairing.

Context: The wisdom literature of the Bible often summarises the realities of life: it can be hard to keep hoping when one's hopes are confounded.

> Proverbs 13.12
> *Hope deferred maketh the heart sick: But when the desire cometh, it is a tree of life.*

how the mighty have fallen

Usage: Used in situations where expectations have not been met by people who promised much.

Context: David laments the death of Saul and Jonathan in battle. Saul was David's enemy for much of his life yet David recognises that he was a great man.

> 2 Samuel 1.19
> *The beauty of Israel is slain upon thy high places: How are the mighty fallen!*

Ichabod

Usage: Literally 'the glory has departed' so refers to anything that has declined or failed.

Context: The wife of Phinehas, son of Eli, the priest names her child Ichabod because she hears of the defeat of Israel and the capture of the Ark of the Covenant (the symbol of God's presence or his glory) as she is giving birth.

> 1 Samuel 4.21
> *And she named the child I-chabod, saying, The glory is departed from Israel: because the ark of God was taken, and because of her father in law and her husband.*

if you're not with me you're against me

Usage: Indifference to a cause can be as unsupportive as outright opposition.

Context: Jesus teaches that no one can be indifferent to him; being indifferent to him is the same as opposing him.

> Matthew 12.30
> *He that is not with me is against me; and he that gathereth not with me scattereth abroad.*

in the beginning

Usage: One of the most well-known phrases from the Bible, used at the start of speeches, articles, etc., adapted to fit the relevant topic; the phrase was used by Hazel O'Connor in her song 'Eighth Day' which satirises humankind's destruction of the environment.

Context: The start of Genesis describes how God ceated the world. Its first words are 'In the beginning God' which is echoed at the start of John's gospel which starts 'In the beginning was the Word ... '.

> Genesis 1.1 see also John 1.1
> *In the beginning God created the heaven and the earth.*

in the twinkling of an eye

Usage: Something that happens very quickly, in an instant; used by William Shakespeare in the *Merchant of Venice* in the phrase 'I'll take my leave of the Jew in the twinkling of an eye.'

Context: The phrase is used by Paul to refer to future events that will happen so quickly that no one will have time to think about it.

> 1 Corinthians 15.52
> *in a moment, in the twinkling of an eye, at the last trump: for the trumpet shall sound, and the dead shall be raised incorruptible, and we shall be changed.*

issue of blood

Usage: Bleeding, usually from a wound.

Context: A woman who is ritually unclean according to Jewish law touches Jesus and is healed. Jesus ignores the ritual laws in caring for the woman.

> Matthew 9.20
> *And, behold, a woman, which was diseased with an issue of blood twelve years, came behind him, and touched the hem of his garment.*

Jacob's ladder

Usage: A steep set of stairs or used in a specialised sense of a ship's rope ladder; a popular Negro spiritual song; title of a film by Adrian Lyne (1990).

Context: Jacob's dream of angels ascending and descending reveals to him that the realms of heaven and earth are closer and more interlocking than he had thought. God speaks to him and renews the promise he had made to Jacob's father, Isaac, and grandfather, Abraham, to give him the land on which he was lying.

> **Genesis 28.12**
> *And he dreamed, and behold a ladder set up on the earth, and the top of it reached to heaven: and behold the angels of God ascending and descending on it.*

Jesus wept

Usage: Often an imprecation or exclamation.

Context: The shortest verse in the KJV. Jesus is deeply moved by the death of his friend Lazarus and cries at his tomb before raising him from the dead.

> **John 11.35**
> *Jesus wept.*

Jezebel

Usage: A woman of loose morals and scheming character; the title of film starring Bette Davis (1938).

Context: Jezebel and Ahab worshipped the god Baal and opposed and plotted to kill God's prophet Elijah. Baal-worship varied but included fertility rituals of a sexual nature.

> **1 Kings 16.31**
> *And it came to pass, as if it had been a light thing for him to walk in the sins of Jeroboam the son of Nebat, that he took to wife Jezebel the daughter of Ethbaal king of the Zidonians, and went and served Baal, and worshipped him.*

Job's comforters

Usage: People who mean well but make someone suffering feel worse; see also 'patience of Job'.

Context: Job is a righteous man who is allowed by God to suffer the loss of family possessions and health. His friends argue that as God is just he must deserve his suffering. Job argues that suffering is not always deserved and is not in his case.

> **Job 2.11 see also Job 16.2**
> *Now when Job's three friends heard of all this evil that was come upon him, they came every one from his own place; Eliphaz the Temanite, and Bildad the Shuhite, and Zophar the Naamathite: for they had made an appointment together to come to mourn with him, and to comfort him.*

Jonah

Usage: Someone who brings bad luck.

Context: Jonah tries to evade God's call to preach to the heathens of Nineveh by taking a ship in the opposite direction. He tells the sailors that the storm which is breaking up their ship is his fault. They throw him overboard and the storm subsides, leaving Jonah to be ferried to Nineveh in the stomach of a fish or whale.

> **Jonah 1.13–17**
> *Nevertheless the men rowed hard to bring it to the land; but they could not: for the sea wrought, and was tempestuous against them. Wherefore they cried unto the LORD, and said, We beseech thee, O LORD, we beseech thee, let us not perish for this man's life, and lay not upon us innocent blood: for thou, O LORD, hast done as it pleased thee. So they took up Jonah, and cast him forth into the sea: and the sea ceased from her raging. Then the men feared the LORD exceedingly, and offered a sacrifice unto the LORD, and made vows. Now the LORD had prepared a great fish to swallow up Jonah. And Jonah was in the belly of the fish three days and three nights.*

Jubilee

Usage: A major anniversary, e.g. Queen's Silver Jubilee, a golden jubilee.

Context: The jubilee was named after the ram's horn trumpet which was sounded to announce the festival of the fiftieth year in Jewish tradition. It was a time of joy and celebration, the freeing of slaves and the return of property.

> **Leviticus 25.10**
> *And ye shall hallow the fiftieth year, and proclaim liberty throughout all the land unto all the inhabitants thereof: it shall be a jubile unto you; and ye shall return every man unto his possession, and ye shall return every man unto his family.*

Judas

Usage: One who betrays another.

Context: Judas Iscariot was one of Jesus' close followers but took money from the Jewish religious leaders to betray Jesus. The agreed sign was a kiss of greeting hence also 'to betray with a kiss' is a byword for using a sign of love to betray someone.

> **Matthew 10.4**
> *Simon the Canaanite, and Judas Iscariot, who also betrayed him.*

keeping the best until last

Usage: Holding back the best thing one has to offer until the last minute.

Context: At the wedding in Cana Jesus turned water into wine. The leader of the feast (equivalent to the best man) tasted the miraculous wine and concluded that, contrary to usual practice, the best had been kept until last.

> **John 2.10**
> *and saith unto him, Every man at the beginning doth set forth good wine; and when men have well drunk, then that which is worse: but thou hast kept the good wine until now.*

kind word turns away anger

Usage: Gracious words spoken to an angry person can defuse their anger.

Context: The modern proverb is probably a conflation of the two parts of the verse; the same process happens in 'pride goes before a fall'.

> **Proverbs 15.1**
> *A soft answer turneth away wrath: But grievous words stir up anger.*

labourer is worthy of his hire

Usage: Workers deserve payment.

Context: Jesus sends out the disciples to teach and he tells them to rely on people seeing that their message is valuable and thus the preachers are worthy of support.

> **Luke 10.7**
> *And in the same house remain, eating and drinking such things as they give: for the labourer is worthy of his hire. Go not from house to house.*

lamb to the slaughter

Usage: An innocent or defenceless victim.

Context: The phrase is used of the Servant of the Lord in the prophecy of Isaiah. Christian tradition interpreted the Servant as prefiguring Jesus.

> **Isaiah 53.7**
> *He was oppressed, and he was afflicted, yet he opened not his mouth: he is brought as a lamb to the slaughter, and as a sheep before her shearers is dumb, so he openeth not his mouth.*

land flowing with milk and honey

Usage: A place where the good things of life are freely and effortlessly available.

Context: As a nomadic tribe of herdsmen the early Israelites valued the produce of their herds and the bounty of the country in honey. This then is a picture of an idyllic land good for sheep and rich with bees.

> **Exodus 3.8**
> *and I am come down to deliver them out of the hand of the Egyptians, and to bring them up out of that land unto a good land and a large, unto a land flowing with milk and honey; unto the place of the Canaanites, and the Hittites, and the Amorites, and the Perizzites, and the Hivites, and the Jebusites.*

land of the living

Usage: Often used to describe a return of attention to the present moment.

Context: This phrase is used 15 times in the Old Testament to contrast the life now with death.

> **Job 28.13 see also Psalm 27.13, 52.5; Isaiah 38.11; Jeremiah 11.19; Ezekiel 32.23–27**
> *Man knoweth not the price thereof; Neither is it found in the land of the living.*

land of Nod

Usage: A juvenile term for sleep first used by Jonathan Swift; the name of a place in East Yorkshire; a play on words associated with nodding off to sleep.

Context: The place is symbolic of exile since it is where Cain was banished to after killing Abel. It may also be symbolic of no fixed abode, i.e. a wanderer welcomed by nobody.

> **Genesis 4.16**
> *And Cain went out from the presence of the LORD, and dwelt in the land of Nod, on the east of Eden.*

last enemy

Usage: A reference to death; title of book by H. Beam Piper (1950).

Context: This reference is part of Paul's argument for the resurrection of the dead. Christ will rule for eternity, all his enemies will be subdued and death itself will be conquered as Christ's resurrection demonstrates.

> **1 Corinthians 15.26**
> *The last enemy that shall be destroyed is death.*

last trump / trumpet

Usage: A signal announcing a climactic change; title of book by Isaac Asimov (1957).

Context: Trumpets announce war or a royal arrival: Christ's victory at the end of time is announced by trumpets and the blast has both these functions.

> **1 Corinthians 15.52**
> *in a moment, in the twinkling of an eye, at the last trump: for the trumpet shall sound, and the dead shall be raised incorruptible, and we shall be changed.*

law of Medes and Persians

Usage: Unchangeable practice often used ironically of the habits of people set in their ways.

Context: The Medes and Persians were famous for the rigidity of their laws.

> **Esther 1.19 see also Daniel 6.8**
> *If it please the king, let there go a royal commandment from him, and let it be written among the laws of the Persians and the Medes, that it be not altered, That Vashti come no more before king Ahasuerus; and let the king give her royal estate unto another that is better than she.*

left hand not knowing what the right is doing

Usage: To do something with good motives and without calculation. Can also be used negatively to imply that someone or an organisation is uninformed of what others are doing.

Context: Jesus advises that good impulses should be given free rein; one should not give with one hand and take back with the other.

> **Matthew 6.3**
> *But when thou doest alms, let not thy left hand know what thy right hand doeth.*

leopard can't change its spots

Usage: Old habits die hard.

Context: Jeremiah suggests that his people are so used to doing evil that it has become their very nature; they can no more change than a leopard can.

> **Jeremiah 13.23**
> *Can the Ethiopian change his skin, or the leopard his spots? then may ye also do good, that are accustomed to do evil.*

let my people go

Usage: A theme in Negro spirituals.

Context: The Israelites are kept in slavery in Egypt and God sends a message through Moses to Pharaoh that he should release them.

Exodus 5.1
And afterward Moses and Aaron went in, and told Pharaoh, Thus saith the LORD God of Israel, Let my people go, that they may hold a feast unto me in the wilderness.

let your 'Yes' be 'Yes' and your 'No' be 'No'

Usage: Also known as 'yea' and 'nay'; an exhortation to be honest and straightforward.

Context: Jesus teaches that honest speech needs no reinforcement from oaths and this teaching is echoed by James.

> **Matthew 5.37 see also James 5.12**
> *But let your communication be, Yea, yea; Nay, nay: for whatsoever is more than these cometh of evil.*

leviathan

Usage: Refers to any big creature or powerful machine, usually of a type associated with water; the name of a book by Thomas Hobbes (1651) on political philosophy.

Context: Leviathan is a water monster, but the Bible references suggest that the name was given to various types of water creature, from the crocodile to the whale.

> **Job 41.1 see also Psalm 74.14, 104.26; Isaiah 27.1**
> *Canst thou draw out leviathan with an hook? Or his tongue with a cord which thou lettest down?*

like a thief in the night

Usage: an event that happens unexpectedly and unpredictably, such as sudden death.

Context: Jesus explains that a watchman does not know at what time of night a thief may or may not come. In the New Testament this metaphor is used of Christ's second coming.

> **Matthew 24.43 see also Luke 12.39;**
> **1 Thessalonians 5.2; 2 Peter 3.10**
> *But know this, that if the goodman of the house had known in what watch the thief would come, he would have watched, and would not have suffered his house to be broken up.*

like mother, like daughter

Usage: Children tend to reproduce the habits of their parents. A variation could be: 'Like father, like son.'

Context: Ezekiel preaches against Jerusalem, characterising Jerusalem and Israel as the daughter of the Hittites. The thrust of his message is that as the parent nation was pagan and idolatrous, so is Israel.

> **Ezekiel 16.44**
> *Behold, every one that useth proverbs shall use this proverb against thee, saying, As is the mother, so is her daughter.*

lilies of the field

Usage: An image of uncultivated natural beauty; title of a book by William Edmund Barrett (1962) and subsequent film.

Context: Jesus teaches that God cares for people more that the rest of his creation and that they can trust him to supply their needs.

> **Matthew 6.28–29**
> *And why take ye thought for raiment? Consider the lilies of the field, how they grow; they toil not, neither do they spin: and yet I say unto you, That even Solomon in all his glory was not arrayed like one of these.*

lion's den

Usage: A gathering of enemies into which a person is precipitated; a variation is 'dragon's den', as in the BBC television series featuring potential entrepreneurs in a room with successful business people.

Context: A literal gruesome punishment to be carried out on anyone who failed to comply with the plan devised by plotters against Daniel. They were attempting to undermine Daniel by making his prayer to God a form of rebellion against the king.

> **Daniel 6.7**
> *All the presidents of the kingdom, the governors, and the princes, the counsellors, and the captains, have consulted together to establish a royal statute, and to make a firm decree, that whosoever shall ask a petition of any God or man for thirty days, save of thee, O king, he shall be cast into the den of lions.*

little leaven

Usage: Usually refers to a process of seasoning, or adding a small measure of something to an undifferentiated mass of something else to improve it.

Context: Leaven is yeast which is a living organism and spreads through dough, producing gas which makes the bread rise. It was especially removed during the Passover feast to symbolise purification. It is used metaphorically as an image of a bad habit which spreads and grows if unchecked.

> **Galatians 5.9**
> *A little leaven leaveneth the whole lump.*

the Lord giveth and the Lord taketh away

Usage: Benefits of life are transient and beyond the understanding of humans; part of the Burial Service of the Book of Common Prayer.

Context: Job has lost everything he has, including his children, but even in this extremity he sees that everything he had was a gift from God.

> **Job 1.21**
> *and said, Naked came I out of my mother's womb, and naked shall I return thither: the LORD gave, and the LORD hath taken away; blessed be the name of the LORD.*

lost sheep

Usage: Someone who feels themselves to be out of their depth and so confused or stupid like a sheep; perhaps following the bad example of others.

Context: Sheep were and are proverbial for getting themselves lost or into danger.

> **Psalm 119.176 see also Jeremiah 50.6; Matthew 10.5-6**
> *I have gone astray like a lost sheep; seek thy servant; For I do not forget thy commandments.*

Lot's wife

Usage: Someone who habitually looks back at the good old days.

Context: The two neighbouring towns of Sodom and Gomorrah were destroyed by God because of their sin. At their destruction Lot and his family were spared but ordered not to look back as the destruction took place; Lot's wife did look back and was also destroyed.

> **Genesis 19.26**
> *But his wife looked back from behind him, and she became a pillar of salt.*

love covers a multitude of sins

Usage: Often used of romantic love where one partner forgives the other.

Context: Peter recognises that the people to whom he is writing come from a thoroughly pagan background and urges the Church to love and forgive each other because they themselves have been loved and forgiven: love covers over past wrongdoing.

> **1 Peter 4.8**
> *And above all things have fervent charity among yourselves: for charity shall cover the multitude of sins.*

love is ...

Usage: A popular cartoon cliché.

Context: Paul describes the love of God (agape) which is worked out and reproduced in Christians. He uses a series of phrases all starting 'love is ...' or 'charity is ...' as in the KJV.

> **1 Corinthians 13.4–8**
> *Charity suffereth long, and is kind; charity envieth not; charity vaunteth not itself, is not puffed up, doth not behave itself unseemly, seeketh not her own, is not easily provoked, thinketh no evil; rejoiceth not in iniquity, but rejoiceth in the truth; beareth all things, believeth all things, hopeth all things, endureth all things. Charity never faileth: but whether there be prophecies, they shall fail; whether there be tongues, they shall cease; whether there be knowledge, it shall vanish away.*

love is strong as death

Usage: A symbol of the strength of someone's love.

Context: The Song of Solomon is love poetry: here the beloved urges her lover to cleave to her with undying love.

> **Song of Solomon 8.6**
> *Set me as a seal upon thine heart, As a seal upon thine arm: For love is strong as death; Jealousy is cruel as the grave: The coals thereof are coals of fire,*

love thy neighbour (as thyself)

Usage: The need to love everyone.

Context: In Leviticus the command is related to the principle of vengeance: people should not avenge wrongs done to them by their fellow-Israelites by taking the law into their own hands. In the New Testament, Jesus explains that the greatest commandments are to love God and to 'love thy neighbour as thyself'. Using the parable of the Good Samaritan, he then defines neighbour as anyone in need. It is later emphasised by Paul and James in letters.

> **Leviticus 19.18 see also Matthew 22.39;**
> **Galatians 5.14; James 2.8**
> *Thou shalt not avenge, nor bear any grudge against the children of thy people, but thou shalt love thy neighbour as thyself: I am the LORD.*

love your enemies

Usage: The need to love even those who seek to wrong a person.

Context: Jesus asks that his followers show the same kind of love to others as God has shown to them, regardless of how they are treated in return.

> **Luke 6.27**
> *But I say unto you which hear, Love your enemies, do good to them which hate you,*

making bricks without straw

Usage: Doing a job without proper equipment or materials.

Context: Pharaoh cruelly denies the Israelite slaves the basic materials for their work but demands the same output.

> **Exodus 5.7**
> *Ye shall no more give the people straw to make brick, as heretofore: let them go and gather straw for themselves.*

man after [someone's] own heart

Usage: Someone whose attitudes one deeply approves of and whose values correspond with one's own.

Context: King Saul repeatedly fails to do what God asks of him so Samuel is commissioned to look for the future leader who will do God's will. He anoints David.

> **1 Samuel 13.14**
> *But now thy kingdom shall not continue: the LORD hath sought him a man after his own heart, and the LORD hath commanded him to be captain over his people, because thou hast not kept that which the LORD commanded thee.*

man is born to trouble

Usage: An acknowledgement of the sentiment that difficult times are experienced by every person.

Context: Job argues that trouble and hardship are not necessary or inevitable and yet they appear to happen regularly and naturally as part of everyday experience.

> **Job 5.7**
> *Yet man is born unto trouble, As the sparks fly upward.*

man of sorrows

Usage: Perhaps someone having much grief and hardship.

Context: The passage describes the 'Servant of the Lord' who suffers on behalf of others. Christians understand it to refer to Jesus.

Isaiah 53.3
He is despised and rejected of men; a man of sorrows, and acquainted with grief: and we hid as it were our faces from him; he was despised, and we esteemed him not.

man shall not live by bread alone

Usage: There are more important things in life than the merely physical.

Context: Jesus echoes the teaching in Deuteronomy that it is God who sustains life with his word and power, not food alone. Jesus, during his 40-day fast, was being tempted to make stones into bread by the devil.

Deuteronomy 8.3 see also Matthew 4.4
And he humbled thee, and suffered thee to hunger, and fed thee with manna, which thou knewest not, neither did thy fathers know; that he might make thee know that man doth not live by bread only, but by every word that proceedeth out of the mouth of the LORD doth man live.

manna [bread] from heaven

Usage: Something unexpectedly, freely or unstintingly given; 'bread of heaven' is a line from the Welsh hymn 'Guide Me O Thou Great Jehovah'.

Context: God provided food for the Israelites in the barren wilderness for forty years in the form of manna.

Nehemiah 9.15 see also Exodus 16.4–15; John 6.32
And gavest them bread from heaven for their hunger, and broughtest forth water for them out of the rock for their thirst, and promisedst them that they should go in to possess the land which thou hadst sworn to give them.

many are called, but few are chosen

Usage: Lots of people might desire or want something but only a few are suitable to receive it.

Context: In a parable, Jesus has spoken of a king who invites many people to his wedding banquet; those who accept properly are given special clothing and anyone without such clothing is a gatecrasher. So the invitation is to all, but guests have to accept.

Matthew 22.14
For many are called, but few are chosen.

many mansions

Usage: Room enough for everyone; particularly used of heaven for all who are worthy.

Context: Jesus speaks of heaven where he goes to prepare rich habitations for his disciples.

> **John 14.2**
> *In my Father's house are many mansions: if it were not so, I would have told you. I go to prepare a place for you.*

many waters cannot quench love

Usage: Love is unconquerable.

Context: The Song of Solomon is love poetry: the lovers praise the power and strength of true love.

> **Song of Solomon 8.7**
> *Many waters cannot quench love, Neither can the floods drown it: If a man would give all the substance of his house for love, It would utterly be contemned.*

mark of Cain

Usage: Usually metaphorically applied to someone who is habitually bad; *Kane and Abel* was a novel by Jeffrey Archer which played on this theme.

Context: Cain is punished and exiled from Eden for killing his brother Abel. The mark put on him protects him from being killed so that he can serve the full sentence.

> **Genesis 4.15**
> *And the LORD said unto him, Therefore whosoever slayeth Cain, vengeance shall be taken on him sevenfold. And the LORD set a mark upon Cain, lest any finding him should kill him.*

mark of the Beast

Usage: Usually metaphorically applied to someone who is habitually wicked.

Context: The Beast is an opponent of God in Revelation. He puts a distinguishing mark on his followers who worship him, though various numbers and designs have been associated with the Beast.

> **Revelation 16.2**
> *And the first went, and poured out his vial upon the earth; and there fell a noisome and grievous sore upon the men which had the mark of the beast, and upon them which worshipped his image.*

mess of pottage

Usage: Greatly desired but of little value for which one gives away something precious.

Context: Esau was so hungry and impatient for food that he gave away his rights of inheritance to his brother in return for a stew.

Genesis 25.34
*Then Jacob gave Esau bread and pottage of lentiles;
and he did eat and drink, and rose up, and went
his way: thus Esau despised his birthright.*

millstone around one's neck

Usage: Something that drags one down and prevents
one from achieving things.

Context: Jesus teaches that children are especially
precious to him. He states that for those who injure
or corrupt them it would be better if a millstone
were hung around their neck and they were cast
into the sea. The theme is continued in Revelation
where the writer uses the same term for the sinful
city of Babylon.

**Matthew 18.6; Mark 9.42; Luke 17.2;
Revelation 18.21–22**
*But whoso shall offend one of these little ones
which believe in me, it were better for him that a
millstone were hanged about his neck, and that
he were drowned in the depth of the sea.*

(love of) money is the root of all evil

Usage: A comment on an evil action where financial
gain is considered the primary underlying cause.

Context: The Bible states that the love of money is
the root of all evil, rather than money itself: people
will do all kinds of wicked things for money.

1 Timothy 6.10
*For the love of money is the root of all evil: which
while some coveted after, they have erred from
the faith, and pierced themselves through with
many sorrows.*

more blessed to give than to receive

Usage: The paradoxical experience that one's own
life can be enhanced when we give generously to
others.

Context: Paul reminds the Ephesians whom he is
visiting that Jesus taught his followers to help each
other generously and said they would find blessing
in doing so. This saying of Jesus is not found in the
Gospels but is consistent with his teaching there.

Acts 20.35
*I have shewed you all things, how that so labouring
ye ought to support the weak, and to remember
the words of the Lord Jesus, how he said, It is more
blessed to give than to receive.*

Moses basket

Usage: A basketwork carry-cot for babies.

Context: Moses is saved from Pharaoh's plan to reduce the Israelites' threat by killing baby boys. Moses' mother floats him on the river in a basket. He is found by Pharaoh's daughter and she who adopts him.

> **Exodus 2.3**
> *And when she could not longer hide him, she took for him an ark of bulrushes, and daubed it with slime and with pitch, and put the child therein; and she laid it in the flags by the river's brink.*

mote (speck) in the eye

Usage: A minor flaw in someone's character or behaviour.

Context: One of Jesus' homely images in the Sermon on the Mount, this saying advocates humility and a greater sensitivity to one's own sin than to that of others. Jesus the carpenter would have been very familiar with dust and planks.

> **Matthew 7.3**
> *And why beholdest thou the mote that is in thy brother's eye, but considerest not the beam that is in thine own eye?*

my cup runneth over

Usage: I have more than enough for my needs.

Context: In Psalm 23 the psalmist writes that God was preparing a table and was so generous that his cup ran over, presumably with wine.

> **Psalm 23.5**
> *Thou preparest a table before me in the presence of mine enemies: Thou anointest my head with oil; my cup runneth over.*

new Jerusalem

Usage: A vision of hope and renewal; mentioned in William Blake's poem *Jerusalem*.

Context: The New Testament frequently refers to a time when God will remake the earth: Jerusalem, the city where God's name is particularly honoured, becomes an image of the new world order where God is honoured for ever.

> **Revelation 3.12**
> *Him that overcometh will I make a pillar in the temple of my God, and he shall go no more out: and I will write upon him the name of my God, and the name of the city of my God, which is new Jerusalem, which cometh down out of heaven from my God: and I will write upon him my new name.*

Nimrod

Usage: Someone with a reputation for hunting and, by extension, violence; the name of one of Elgar's *Enigma Variations* (1899) music for AJ Jaeger (the surname is German for 'hunter'); in Dante's *Divine Comedy*, Nimrod is a figure in the Inferno; the name of an aeroplane used by the Royal Air Force.

Context: A mighty hunter, one of the descendants of Cush, son of Noah.

> **Genesis 10.8–9**
> *And Cush begat Nimrod: he began to be a mighty one in the earth. He was a mighty hunter before the LORD: wherefore it is said, Even as Nimrod the mighty hunter before the LORD.*

no abiding city

Usage: A reference to a sense that things are transient and do not last or stay the same.

Context: The New Testament frequently refers to a time when God will remake the earth: Jerusalem, the city where God's name is particularly honoured, becomes an image of the new world order where God is honoured forever. This is the city for which Christians long.

> **Hebrews 13.14**
> *For here have we no continuing city, but we seek one to come.*

no bigger than a man's fist hand

Usage: An apparently insignificant sign heralds a significant or long-awaited change; used to refer to small things such as kittens.

Context: After three years of drought in Israel the prophet Elijah prophesied that God would send rain. He sends his servant out seven times to look for the rain and the seventh time he makes this report. The cloud presages the fulfilment of the prophecy.

> **1 Kings 18.44**
> *And it came to pass at the seventh time, that he said, Behold, there ariseth a little cloud out of the sea, like a man's hand. And he said, Go up, say unto Ahab, Prepare thy chariot, and get thee down, that the rain stop thee not.*

no respecter of persons

Usage: Someone or something that does not make distinctions between people.

Context: Peter addresses a Gentile group at the house of Cornelius, a Roman centurion. As a Jew he was uneasy about consorting with Gentiles until

God gives him a vision and sends him to preach to these people.

> **Acts 10.34**
> *Then Peter opened his mouth, and said, Of a truth I perceive that God is no respecter of persons.*

no room at the inn

Usage: Jocularly used to mean no room anywhere.

Context: In Christian tradition, Jesus is said to have been born in a stable because there was no room left for people at the inns of Bethlehem.

> **Luke 2.7**
> *And she brought forth her firstborn son, and wrapped him in swaddling clothes, and laid him in a manger; because there was no room for them in the inn.*

O death where is thy sting

Usage: There is no need to be scared of dying.

Context: The resurrection of Jesus makes it clear that death is not the end and thus the venomous snake-bite that is death is not terminal. Death does not win in the end.

> **1 Corinthians 15.55**
> *O death, where is thy sting? O grave, where is thy victory?*

O ye of little faith

Usage: Said to people fearful or doubtful of the outcome of some project.

Context: Nature shows God's care and control of the world, so human beings should trust him to look after them too.

> **Matthew 6.30**
> *Wherefore, if God so clothe the grass of the field, which to day is, and to morrow is cast into the oven, shall he not much more clothe you, O ye of little faith?*

of making many books there is no end

Usage: Any student knows that writing can become tedious.

Context: It is hard to interpret the context of this saying at the end of Ecclesiastes: it might mean that practical wisdom is better than book learning or that already the book is too long. Whatever else it might mean, it signals the end of the book and the argument.

Ecclesiastes 12.12
And further, by these, my son, be admonished: of making many books there is no end; and much study is a weariness of the flesh.

offscouring of all things

Usage: Rubbish like filth to be scraped off the skin.

Context: Paul describes his ministry and the ill-treatment he receives and compares that with the relative comfort of the Corinthians. Paul has no concern for status and repays evil for good.

1 Corinthians 4.13 see also Lamentations 3.45
being defamed, we intreat: we are made as the filth of the world, and are the offscouring of all things unto this day.

oil of gladness

Usage: Used to anoint sweet smelling oils denoting God's love.

Context: An image of harmony oil was used in ceremonies of ordination, reconciliation and blessing.

Psalm 45.7 see also Hebrews 1.9
Thou lovest righteousness, and hatest wickedness: Therefore God, thy God, hath anointed thee with the oil of gladness above thy fellows.

old Adam

Usage: A reference to degenerate human nature, humanity without Christ.

Context: Adam's human sin brought about the alienation of humanity from God; Christ's human obedience brought about the reconciliation of humanity and God. Adam was the first human and disobeyed God's command; Christ was the first human to obey God's will perfectly.

1 Corinthians 15.45
And so it is written, The first man Adam was made a living soul; the last Adam was made a quickening spirit.

old as Methuselah

Usage: An image of extreme age.

Context: Methuselah was the person who had the longest life of all those recorded in the Bible – 969 years.

Genesis 5.27
and all the days of Methuselah were nine hundred sixty and nine years: and he died.

on one's own head

Usage: When one takes full responsibility for one's decisions or receives the (unpleasant) results of one's actions.

Context: The psalmist rejoices in the justice of God, which means that people's tricks misfire. Paul's speech records his decision to preach to the Gentiles rather than to the Jews who have opposed and persecuted him.

> **Psalm 7.16 see also Acts 18.6**
> *His mischief shall return upon his own head, And his violent dealing shall come down upon his own pate.*

open sepulchre

Usage: Used to describe a hypocrite; to be foul-mouthed.

Context: In the heat of the Middle East it was important that dead bodies were quickly entombed (a sepulchre is a tomb) as decay would soon commence. The psalmist likens the speech of the wicked to an open sepulchre revealing the corruption within.

> **Psalm 5.9**
> *For there is no faithfulness in their mouth; Their inward part is very wickedness; Their throat is an open sepulchre; They flatter with their tongue.*

out of the Ark

Usage: Jocularly used of something very old or outdated, which has survived the wretches of time and somehow been saved.

Context: Noah, his family and the animals from the Ark repopulated the earth after the flood having been saved from destruction by the Ark. While not as early as Adam and Eve, they are symbolic of ancient times and practices.

> **Genesis 8.19**
> *every beast, every creeping thing, and every fowl, and whatsoever creepeth upon the earth, after their kinds, went forth out of the ark.*

out of the depths

Usage: Refers particularly to (the cry of) those in deep distress. The translation of the Latin Vulgate Bible *De profundis* is used in art music and literature, e.g. Oscar Wilde's poem of that name.

Context: The psalm originally seems to refer to the psalmist's penitence rather than primarily his feelings of misery but it undoubtedly suits both.

> **Psalm 130.1**
> *Out of the depths have I cried unto thee, O LORD.*

out of the mouths of babes and sucklings

Usage: Usually an exclamation referring to unexpectedly precocious knowledge or insight.

Context: The Bible passages suggest that the young and relatively innocent recognise and reflect spiritual truth that older people either do not want or do not wish to.

> **Psalm 8.2 see also Matthew 21.16**
> *Out of the mouth of babes and sucklings hast thou ordained strength because of thine enemies, That thou mightest still the enemy and the avenger.*

out of the strong came forth sweetness

Usage: A paradox paraphrased by sugar refiners Tate and Lyle in their trade mark.

Context: Part of a riddle set by Samson for the Philistine guests at his wedding and based on his finding a nest of bees in the carcass of a lion he had killed; Samson's wife wheedles the answer out of him and gives it away.

> **Judges 14.14**
> *And he said unto them, Out of the eater came forth meat, And out of the strong came forth sweetness. And they could not in three days expound the riddle.*

paid the last penny

Usage: Fully paid with nothing omitted; *Not a Penny More, Not a Penny Less* is the title of a novel by Jeffrey Archer (1976).

Context: Jesus teaches that a conciliatory attitude is best; if someone takes matters to court the case may be decided in favour of the opponent and the costs will have to be fully paid by the person who took the matter too far.

> **Matthew 5.26 see also Luke 12.59**
> *Verily I say unto thee, Thou shalt by no means come out thence, till thou hast paid the uttermost farthing.*

painted Jezebel

Usage: A prostitute or scheming woman; see also 'Jezebel'.

Context: This is Jezebel's last action before she is killed. She seems either to be trying to impress the warlike Jehu or preparing for her death. She is thrown out of the window.

2 Kings 9.30
And when Jehu was come to Jezreel, Jezebel heard of it; and she painted her face, and tired her head, and looked out at a window.

parting of the ways

Usage: A difficult decision, often relating to relationships where one party wants something different from the other.

Context: The king of Babylon uses divination to decide which way to take his army to attack Jerusalem or another place. Here the phrase means a road which divides.

Ezekiel 21.21
For the king of Babylon stood at the parting of the way, at the head of the two ways, to use divination: he made his arrows bright, he consulted with images, he looked in the liver.

pass by on the other side

Usage: To take no notice of someone who needs your help, sometimes literally crossing the road to avoid them.

Context: In Jesus' parable of the Good Samaritan, the man who lay injured by the side of the road was ignored by religious men who would have been expected to help him.

Luke 10.31–32
And by chance there came down a certain priest that way: and when he saw him, he passed by on the other side. And likewise a Levite, when he was at the place, came and looked on him, and passed by on the other side.

passing (exceeding) the love of woman

Usage: Something more delightful than romantic love.

Context: David laments the death of Jonathan, his dearest friend who had valued and loved him more than any woman.

2 Samuel 1.26
I am distressed for thee, my brother Jonathan: Very pleasant hast thou been unto me: Thy love to me was wonderful, Passing the love of women.

patience of Job

Usage: Remarkable perseverance or patience.

Context: Job was tested by the loss of everything he valued but refused to deny his faith in God.

James 5.11 see also Job
Behold, we count them happy which endure. Ye have heard of the patience of Job, and have seen

*the end of the Lord; that the Lord is very pitiful,
and of tender mercy.*

pearl of great price

Usage: Something to be valued most highly.

Context: One of Jesus' parables of the Kingdom,
he likens the Kingdom of God to various things for
which people might give everything they have or
make extreme acts of sacrifice to possess.

Matthew 13.46
*who, when he had found one pearl of great price,
went and sold all that he had, and bought it.*

Philistine

Usage: Someone who despises culture.

Context: The Philistines were the main opponents
of the Israelites in the early days of the Israelite
monarchy. Their reputation for being opposed to
culture depends on their enmity against Israel.

Judges 13.1
*And the children of Israel did evil again in the sight
of the LORD; and the LORD delivered them into
the hand of the Philistines forty years.*

physician heal thyself

Usage: Someone who claims to be an expert should
be able to solve their own problems.

Context: Jesus gets an initially favourable reception
at Nazareth, his home town, but he perceives that
the people there do not understand how radical his
message is. This is one of several 'medical' sayings
in Luke's Gospel.

Luke 4.23
*And he said unto them, Ye will surely say unto me
this proverb, Physician, heal thyself: whatsoever
we have heard done in Capernaum, do also here
in thy country.*

pillar of cloud / fire

Usage: Used literally of a column of flame or smoke,
or metaphorically of eye-catching or obvious signs
or pointers.

Context: God guides and protects the people of Israel
by these means as they wander in the wilderness;
may refer to the sight of distant volcanic eruption.

Exodus 13.21
*And the LORD went before them by day in a pillar
of a cloud, to lead them the way; and by night in
a pillar of fire, to give them light; to go by day
and night.*

plague of locusts

Usage: Used literally of the swarms of locusts that devastate crops in tropical and sub-tropical areas.

Context: This was one of the plagues visited upon the Egyptians because Pharaoh refused to let the people of Israel free from slavery.

> **Exodus 10.12**
> *And the LORD said unto Moses, Stretch out thine hand over the land of Egypt for the locusts, that they may come up upon the land of Egypt, and eat every herb of the land, even all that the hail hath left.*

the poor you always have with you

Usage: Disparity of wealth is a constant feature of human society.

Context: Jesus corrects the disciples for being indignant at a woman pouring expensive ointment on him. Aware of his impending death, Jesus says that they can always look after the poor but will not always be able to do kind actions to him personally.

> **Matthew 26.11**
> *For ye have the poor always with you; but me ye have not always.*

pour out one's heart

Usage: To open up to another person and tell them your thoughts and feelings, often troubles or sorrows.

Context: In the Bible, God pours out his wrath or his fury and later pours out his Spirit on his people. In return God's people pour out the blood of sacrifice or they pour out their hearts in repentance.

> **Psalm 62.8 see also Lamentations 2.19**
> *Trust in him at all times; ye people, Pour out your heart before him:God is a refuge for us.*

power and the glory

Usage: The title of a novel by Graham Greene; a line from the song 'Hymn' by Ultravox (1982).

Context: Traditional in the Lord's Prayer, this phrase is not found in the earliest Gospel manuscripts. It is, however, a fitting conclusion to the prayer in the form of a doxology.

> **Matthew 6.13**
> *And lead us not into temptation, but deliver us from evil: For thine is the kingdom, and the power, and the glory, for ever. Amen.*

powers that be

Usage: Refers to any group that holds authority over another.

Context: In Romans the letter writer explains that every soul should be subject to the higher powers.

Romans 13.1
Let every soul be subject unto the higher powers. For there is no power but of God: the powers that be are ordained of God.

pressing on (towards the goal)

Usage: Urging oneself on; devoting one's energy to finishing something.

Context: The phrase here suggests continuing on a course until the prize has been gained.

Philippians 3.14
I press toward the mark for the prize of the high calling of God in Christ Jesus.

pride comes before a fall

Usage: People who boast set themselves up for failure.

Context: Proverbs is much concerned with practical wisdom and maintaining good relations with others. Here the wisdom of Solomon recommends humility by showing what happens when it is absent.

Proverbs 11.2
When pride cometh, then cometh shame: But with the lowly is wisdom.

prodigal son

Usage: One who cuts loose from all restraint of family and friends.

Context: Jesus tells the story of a son who demands his inheritance before his father dies and goes far away to spend it. He falls on hard times and returns to his father destitute. His father welcomes him back with open arms, imaging God's love and welcome for people who have rebelled against him.

Luke 15.11–32
And he said, A certain man had two sons: and the younger of them said to his father, Father, give me the portion of goods that falleth to me. And he divided unto them his living. And not many days after the younger son gathered all together, and took his journey into a far country, and there wasted his substance with riotous living. And when he had spent all, there arose a mighty famine in that land; and he began to be in want. And he went and joined himself to a citizen of that country; and he sent him into his fields to feed swine. And he would fain have filled his belly with the husks that

the swine did eat: and no man gave unto him. And when he came to himself, he said, How many hired servants of my father's have bread enough and to spare, and I perish with hunger! I will arise and go to my father, and will say unto him, Father, I have sinned against heaven, and before thee, and am no more worthy to be called thy son: make me as one of thy hired servants. And he arose, and came to his father. But when he was yet a great way off, his father saw him, and had compassion, and ran, and fell on his neck, and kissed him. And the son said unto him, Father, I have sinned against heaven, and in thy sight, and am no more worthy to be called thy son. But the father said to his servants, Bring forth the best robe, and put it on him; and put a ring on his hand, and shoes on his feet: and bring hither the fatted calf, and kill it; and let us eat, and be merry: for this my son was dead, and is alive again; he was lost, and is found. And they began to be merry. Now his elder son was in the field: and as he came and drew nigh to the house, he heard musick and dancing. And he called one of the servants, and asked what these things meant. And he said unto him, Thy brother is come; and thy father hath killed the fatted calf, because he hath received him safe and sound. And he was angry, and would not go in: therefore came his father out, and intreated him. And he answering said to his father, Lo, these many years do I serve thee, neither transgressed I at any time thy commandment: and yet thou never gavest me a kid, that I might make merry with my friends: but as soon as this thy son was come, which hath devoured thy living with harlots, thou hast killed for him the fatted calf. And he said unto him, Son, thou art ever with me, and all that I have is thine. It was meet that we should make merry, and be glad: for this thy brother was dead, and is alive again; and was lost, and is found.

promised land

Usage: Used metaphorically of any future happiness, often of heaven; also used by early Puritans to refer to America.

Context: God promised a land to Abraham and his descendants. The promise kept the people together during the wanderings in the wilderness after being freed from slavery in Egypt and was fulfilled when the people settled in the land of Canaan.

Exodus 12.25
And it shall come to pass, when ye be come to the land which the LORD will give you, according as he hath promised, that ye shall keep this service.

prophet without honour in his own country

Usage: Those closest in acquaintance to a person are often most sceptical about claims that person may make.

Context: Jesus is rejected by people of his home town: they refer to his parentage and brothers and sisters, perhaps implying a slur.

> **Matthew 13.57**
> *And they were offended in him. But Jesus said unto them, A prophet is not without honour, save in his own country, and in his own house.*

put words in his / her mouth

Usage: To say what you think someone else means, often incorrectly.

Context: In the Bible, prophets were spokesmen or spokeswomen for God. It was believed that God put words into their mouth to speak.

> **Exodus 4.15 see also Deuteronomy 18.18;**
> **2 Samuel 14.3; 2 Samuel 19; Jeremiah 1.9**
> *And thou shalt speak unto him, and put words in his mouth: and I will be with thy mouth, and with his mouth, and will teach you what ye shall do.*

Queen of Sheba

Usage: Sometimes used jocularly in 'And I'm the Queen of Sheba', i.e. to deny an implausible claim.

Context: A wise and powerful queen who came to learn from Solomon. Sheba was a powerful kingdom, probably in the area of today's Yemen.

> **1 Kings 10.1**
> *And when the queen of Sheba heard of the fame of Solomon concerning the name of the LORD, she came to prove him with hard questions.*

quick and the dead

Usage: Often now used in contexts where quick has its modern meaning 'rapid'; a phrase used as several book and film titles, often associated with gunfighting.

Context: The 'quick' are those who are alive as against those who have died. In the Bible the phrase means 'everyone' dead or alive.

> **Acts 10.42 see also 2 Timothy 4.1; 1 Peter 4.5**
> *And he commanded us to preach unto the people, and to testify that it is he which was ordained of God to be the Judge of quick and dead.*

reaping what one sows

Usage: Refers to the notion that in the end what one does determines what one gets by way of reward.

Context: In Paul's argument love shown to another is never wasted; it is a way of building spiritual character. Failure to behave well to others will lead to negative consequences.

> **Galatians 6.7**
> *Be not deceived; God is not mocked: for whatsoever a man soweth, that shall he also reap.*

red sky at night

Usage: Part of an English weather proverb; 'Red sky at night, shepherd's delight.' Sometimes the same proverb is used with sailors rather than shepherds.

Context: Jesus responds to the demand for a miracle by saying that miracles and signs are all around for those who can see them.

> **Matthew 16.2–3**
> *He answered and said unto them, When it is evening, ye say, It will be fair weather: for the sky is red. And in the morning, It will be foul weather to day: for the sky is red and lowring. O ye hypocrites, ye can discern the face of the sky; but can ye not discern the signs of the times?*

render unto Cæsar

Usage: Pay due regard to rules and regulations, even though you may resent them; also pay money to people that are due it.

Context: Roman taxes were a contentious issue in the time of Jesus. Some people tried to gain a following by advocating non-payment. Jesus makes a clear distinction between those things that are properly due to the state and those things which belong to God.

> **Matthew 22.21**
> *They say unto him, Cæsar's. Then saith he unto them, Render therefore unto Cæsar the things which are Cæsar's; and unto God the things that are God's.*

right hand of fellowship / friendship

Usage: A sign of welcome and co-operation; used in groups to welcome people who join or transfer from another group.

Context: Paul, who has been a savage opponent of the Church, is welcomed by the apostles as a true Christian and fellow-worker.

Galatians 2.9
and when James, Cephas, and John, who seemed to be pillars, perceived the grace that was given unto me, they gave to me and Barnabas the right hands of fellowship; that we should go unto the heathen, and they unto the circumcision.

rule with a rod of iron

Usage: A zero-tolerance approach leadership or management.

Context: Revelation quotes Psalm 2.9. The phrase refers to good and bad rule, in both cases connoting absolute power.

Revelation 2.27
and he shall rule them with a rod of iron; as the vessels of a potter shall they be broken to shivers: even as I received of my Father.

sabbatical

Usage: Time off from the ordinary demands of work (usually following a time of extended service) for reflection and refreshment.

Context: The Sabbath was the day of rest for people and animals instituted by God; as Genesis states, God rested on the seventh day after the previous days of creation.

Leviticus 25.3–4
Six years thou shalt sow thy field, and six years thou shalt prune thy vineyard, and gather in the fruit thereof; but in the seventh year shall be a sabbath of rest unto the land, a sabbath for the LORD: thou shalt neither sow thy field, nor prune thy vineyard.

sackcloth and ashes

Usage: Usually an image of humiliation and remorse.

Context: An outward sign of mourning and repentance throughout Bible times.

Esther 4.3
And in every province, whithersoever the king's commandment and his decree came, there was great mourning among the Jews, and fasting, and weeping, and wailing; and many lay in sackcloth and ashes.

sacrificial lamb

Usage: An innocent or defenceless victim sacrificed although they had personally done nothing wrong.

Context: The Bible takes seriously the offence that sin causes to God. In the Old Testament animals were sacrificed to represent their owner dying in the owner's place so that the owner was 'put right' with God. In the New Testament Jesus is presented as a sacrificial victim who chooses to carry the sins of those who trust in him and so enables them to be reconciled with God.

> **Leviticus 5.6**
> *Speak unto the children of Israel, When a man or woman shall commit any sin that men commit, to do a trespass against the LORD, and that person be guilty;*

safe and sound

Usage: A proverbial variant for 'safe'.

Context: 'Sound' means 'whole uninjured' in the English of the KJV. The father in the parable rejoices that his son comes home with no greater injury than to his pride.

> **Luke 15.27**
> *And he said unto him, Thy brother is come; and thy father hath killed the fatted calf, because he hath received him safe and sound.*

salt of the earth

Usage: A worthy good person.

Context: Salt was very important in the ancient world for preserving, flavour-enhancing and even for payment (whence 'salary'). Jesus' disciples preserve, enliven and enrich the world when they obey him.

> **Matthew 5.13**
> *Ye are the salt of the earth: but if the salt have lost his savour, wherewith shall it be salted? it is thenceforth good for nothing, but to be cast out, and to be trodden under foot of men.*

scales falling from eyes

Usage: A sudden revelation or insight, often into the character of another.

Context: Saul had been blinded in his encounter with the resurrected Christ on the Damascus road. The restoration of his physical sight coincides with the insight that his former life had been opposing God.

> **Acts 9.18**
> *And immediately there fell from his eyes as it had been scales: and he received sight forthwith, and arose, and was baptized.*

scapegoat

Usage: Someone who takes the blame for another's wrongdoing.

Context: The ritual referred to here involves the symbolic transfer of the people's sins to a goat which is then sent out to die, carrying away the sins.

Leviticus 16.10
But the goat, on which the lot fell to be the scapegoat, shall be presented alive before the LORD, to make an atonement with him, and to let him go for a scapegoat into the wilderness.

scarlet woman

Usage: A prostitute or immoral woman.

Context: John might have been describing Rome in the scarlet woman of Revelation.

Revelation 17.4
And the woman was arrayed in purple and scarlet colour, and decked with gold and precious stones and pearls, having a golden cup in her hand full of abominations and filthiness of her fornication.

scribes and Pharisees

Usage: Hypocrites.

Context: Scribes were lawyers: people who could read and write and interpret the law. Pharisees were people who devoted themselves to keeping the law. They were the religious leaders of the time of Jesus but their approach to holiness made it impossible for ordinary people to attain. Thus they are accused of hypocritically keeping God out of the reach of the people. Jesus criticised the Pharisees not because they kept the law, but because they preferred the letter of the law to the spirit of the law.

Matthew 5.20
For I say unto you, That except your righteousness shall exceed the righteousness of the scribes and Pharisees, ye shall in no case enter into the kingdom of heaven.

scum of the earth

Usage: A dismissive and derogatory way of referring to people one does not like or people who do bad things.

Context: Paul describes his ministry and the ill-treatment he receives and compares that with the relative comfort of the Corinthians. Paul has no concern for status and repays evil with good.

1 Corinthians 4.13
being defamed, we intreat: we are made as the filth of the world, and are the offscouring of all things unto this day.

seamless robe

Usage: An image for a complex unity.

Context: The soldiers at the crucifixion fulfil the prophecy of Psalm 22.18: 'They part my garments among them and cast lots upon my vesture.'

> **John 19.23**
> *Then the soldiers, when they had crucified Jesus, took his garments, and made four parts, to every soldier a part; and also his coat: now the coat was without seam, woven from the top throughout.*

seeing the light

Usage: A metaphor for understanding something, usually after a period of bewilderment or indifference.

Context: Light is often used in the Bible for life and insight. The physical light of a lamp represents life lived in a godly way in the world, a life that shines as Jesus' life did.

> **Luke 8.16; Luke 11.33**
> *No man, when he hath lighted a candle, covereth it with a vessel, or putteth it under a bed; but setteth it on a candlestick, that they which enter in may see the light.*

setting one's house in order

Usage: Settling one's affairs before some significant event; other variations include 'keeping one's ...' or 'putting one's ...'.

Context: Hezekiah is instructed to prepare for death but in the event God gives him more time than was at first envisaged.

> **2 Kings 20.1**
> *In those days was Hezekiah sick unto death. And the prophet Isaiah the son of Amoz came to him, and said unto him, Thus saith the LORD, Set thine house in order; for thou shalt die, and not live.*

seven pillars of wisdom

Usage: The title of a book by TE Lawrence (of Arabia).

Context: Seven is the number representing completeness in the Bible. The pillars may be virtues or topics of study but this is uncertain. The pillars fully support Wisdom's house, however.

> **Proverbs 9.1**
> *Wisdom hath builded her house, She hath hewn out her seven pillars.*

shaking the dust off one's feet

Usage: Representing one's rejection and condemnation of someone or something.

Context: This was a graphic representation of being glad to get away from somewhere: shaking the dust off meant one wished for no association with the place to cling to one's person.

> **Matthew 10.14**
> *And whosoever shall not receive you, nor hear your words, when ye depart out of that house or city, shake off the dust of your feet.*

sheep and goats

Usage: Refers to good and bad people respectively.

Context: Sheep and goats were difficult to distinguish in Jesus' time. At the last judgement, however, the true character of people will be revealed through what they have done and God the final judge will reward them appropriately.

> **Matthew 25.32–33**
> *and before him shall be gathered all nations: and he shall separate them one from another, as a shepherd divideth his sheep from the goats: and he shall set the sheep on his right hand, but the goats on the left.*

Shibboleth

Usage: Something, often apparently insignificant, that divides people; often something with no currency; also a word used to tell if someone is local or not.

Context: The men of Gilead fight the men of Ephraim but since they speak the same language some of the defeated men of Ephraim appear the same as the Gileadites. They pronounced words differently, however, and those who pronounced the word Shibboleth in the Ephraimite fashion were slaughtered. One meaning of the word is streams or river. The men were trying to cross the river to get home.

> **Judges 12.6**
> *then said they unto him, Say now Shibboleth: and he said Sibboleth: for he could not frame to pronounce it right. Then they took him, and slew him at the passages of Jordan: and there fell at that time of the Ephraimites forty and two thousand.*

signs of the times

Usage: Indications of the way the wind is blowing, usually with reference to bad things approaching; 'Sign O' the Times' is the title of a song and album by Prince (1987).

Context: Jesus refers to the spiritual state of the world in contrast to the physical state of the weather which is discernible in the sky. He implies that great events are happening and will happen and those with insight can discern the signs.

> **Matthew 16.3**
> *And in the morning, It will be foul weather to day: for the sky is red and lowring. O ye hypocrites, ye can discern the face of the sky; but can ye not discern the signs of the times?*

skin of one's teeth

Usage: A very narrow escape.

Context: Job probably means that his disease is so bad his teeth have fallen out. He now has only his gums.

> **Job 19.20**
> *My bone cleaveth to my skin and to my flesh, And I am escaped with the skin of my teeth.*

Sodom and Gomorrah

Usage: A byword for serious sin, often with a sexual connotation.

Context: The two neighbouring and wealthy towns were destroyed by God because of their sin. Their remains are believed to lie under the Dead Sea.

> **Genesis 19.24**
> *Then the LORD rained upon Sodom and upon Gomorrah brimstone and fire from the LORD out of heaven;*

soft answer turns away anger

Usage: Gentleness diffuses tension.

Context: It is best to be conciliatory.

> **Proverbs 15.1**
> *A soft answer turneth away wrath: But grievous words stir up anger.*

sour grapes

Usage: Bitter comments when one is disappointed in one's own hopes or jealous of another's success; the title of a film by Larry David (1998).

Context: The biblical proverb refers to the perception of the people that they are suffering for the sins of their fathers and forebears. Ezekiel says that this is not the case and that God will hold everyone responsible for their own sin.

Ezekiel 18.2
What mean ye, that ye use this proverb concerning the land of Israel, saying, The fathers have eaten sour grapes, and the children's teeth are set on edge?

sow the wind and reap the whirlwind

Usage: Doing something bad that brings about catastrophic consequences.

Context: The sin and idolatry of Israel bring about the dreadful consequences of oppression and destruction.

Hosea 8.7
For they have sown the wind, and they shall reap the whirlwind: it hath no stalk: the bud shall yield no meal: if so be it yield, the strangers shall swallow it up.

spare the rod and spoil the child

Usage: Undisciplined children are spoilt.

Context: Loving discipline encourages appropriate behaviour. This is a biblical principle that underlies the dealings of God with his people.

Proverbs 13.24
He that spareth his rod hateth his son: But he that loveth him chasteneth him betimes.

spirit is willing but the flesh is weak

Usage: Refers to those who want to do something but cannot quite, perhaps for lack of trying.

Context: Jesus finds his disciples sleeping while he is wrestling with the prospect of his death in the Garden of Gethsemane. He recognises that they want to pray with him but are tired.

Matthew 26.41
Watch and pray, that ye enter not into temptation: the spirit indeed is willing, but the flesh is weak.

stand in awe

Usage: To be spellbound in admiration.

Context: In the psalm the psalmist describes standing in awe of God, which led to wonder and praise.

Psalm 4.4 see also Psalm 33.8; Psalm 119.161
Stand in awe, and sin not: Commune with your own heart upon your bed, and be still.

still small voice

Usage: Often refers to the inward or outward voice of reason or conscience; used by Quakers to refer to the Holy Spirit of God.

Context: Elijah, in deep dejection, is told that God will pass by: a powerful wind, an earthquake and fire smash the mountain around him but they are not God's presence. The 'still small voice' is, and Elijah is encouraged.

1 Kings 19.12
and after the earthquake a fire; but the LORD was not in the fire: and after the fire a still small voice.

sting in the tail

Usage: Something which appears good but has a hidden unpleasant feature or consequence.

Context: The reference in John's apocalyptic vision is to locusts which devastate the land but have additional powers to make people miserable.

Revelation 9.10
And they had tails like unto scorpions, and there were stings in their tails: and their power was to hurt men five months.

stony ground

Usage: Work that does not repay the effort necessary; people who do not respond to approaches.

Context: In Jesus' parable of the sower, the seed represents the gospel message. The people, who are represented by stony ground, respond quickly but superficially to the message.

Mark 4.5
And some fell on stony ground, where it had not much earth; and immediately it sprang up, because it had no depth of earth.

straight and narrow

Usage: Refers to avoidance of crime or misbehaviour for one who has hitherto been guilty.

Context: Jesus teaches that following him is difficult and often means going against one's inclinations.

Matthew 7.14
because strait is the gate, and narrow is the way, which leadeth unto life, and few there be that find it.

strangers and pilgrims

Usage: Refers to a sense of not quite belonging where one is.

Context: In these passages those faithful to God are seen as pilgrims through life with their real home in heaven where their true attachments are.

Hebrews 11.13 see also 1 Peter 2.11
These all died in faith, not having received the promises, but having seen them afar off, and were persuaded of them, and embraced them, and

*confessed that they were strangers and pilgrims
on the earth.*

streets paved with gold

Usage: As in the story of Dick Whittington; the
idea that cities are ostentatiously wealthy or used
metaphorically of the place where one's dreams
will be fulfilled.

Context: The image in Revelation is of extreme
purity and clarity rather than absolute value. The
city of God is a place of light and beauty.

> **Revelation 21.21**
> *And the twelve gates were twelve pearls; every
> several gate was of one pearl: and the street of the
> city was pure gold, as it were transparent glass.*

stumbling block

Usage: An obstacle.

Context: God reveals to Isaiah that he can be
something positive to the people or something
negative depending on how they respond. A stumbling
block was a stone placed in a wrestling ring which
combatants could use to trip their opponent.

> **Isaiah 8.14 see also 1 Peter 2.8**
> *And he shall be for a sanctuary; but for a stone
> of stumbling and for a rock of offence to both the
> houses of Israel, for a gin and for a snare to the
> inhabitants of Jerusalem.*

suffer the little children

Usage: Put up with children and (ironically) with
adults when they behave like them.

Context: In the language of the KJV 'suffer' means
'allow'; so Jesus is saying that the children should
be allowed to come to him and not prevented.

> **Matthew 10.14**
> *But when Jesus saw it, he was much displeased,
> and said unto them, Suffer the little children to
> come unto me, and forbid them not: for of such
> is the kingdom of God.*

sufficient unto the day is the evil thereof

Usage: Refers to a desire to deal with present
problems rather than anticipating future ones.

Context: Jesus urges that kind of trust in God
which leaves the future in his hands and does not
worry unduly.

Matthew 6.34
Take therefore no thought for the morrow: for the morrow shall take thought for the things of itself. Sufficient unto the day is the evil thereof.

sweating blood

Usage: Putting in a great deal of effort.

Context: Jesus, in the Garden of Gethsemane, faces the horrific prospect of his death.

Luke 22.44
And being in an agony he prayed more earnestly: and his sweat was as it were great drops of blood falling down to the ground.

swords into plowshares [ploughshares]

Usage: Put aside enmity.

Context: In Isaiah's prophecy God will bring peace such that weapons will no longer be needed but can be turned to agricultural use.

Isaiah 2.4 see also Micah 4.3
And he shall judge among the nations, and shall rebuke many people: and they shall beat their swords into plowshares, and their spears into pruninghooks: nation shall not lift up sword against nation, neither shall they learn war any more.

taking (someone's) name in vain

Usage: Mocking someone or speaking of them behind their back.

Context: The third of the Ten Commandments, this requires that God's name and character be treated with reverence and respect.

Exodus 20.7 see also Deuteronomy 5.11
Thou shalt not take the name of the LORD thy God in vain; for the LORD will not hold him guiltless that taketh his name in vain.

taking up one's cross

Usage: Putting up with annoyance or deprivation.

Context: Jesus likens following him to willingly preparing for execution.

Matthew 16.24
Then said Jesus unto his disciples, If any man will come after me, let him deny himself, and take up his cross, and follow me.

tell it not in Gath

Usage: Don't mention this, especially to someone who might take pleasure in it.

Context: David laments the death of Saul and Jonathan but does not wish the news to be a cause of rejoicing to their enemies.

2 Samuel 1.19–20
The beauty of Israel is slain upon thy high places: How are the mighty fallen! Tell it not in Gath, Publish it not in the streets of Askelon; Lest the daughters of the Philistines rejoice, Lest the daughters of the uncircumcised triumph.

Ten Commandments

Usage: Laws by which to live a good life.

Context: God's commands through Moses for the ordering of Israelite society. These commandments have been the basis of English law and Christian society since the ninth century AD times.

Exodus 20.1–17
And God spake all these words, saying, I am the LORD thy God, which have brought thee out of the land of Egypt, out of the house of bondage. Thou shalt have no other gods before me. Thou shalt not make unto thee any graven image, or any likeness of any thing that is in heaven above, or that is in the earth beneath, or that is in the water under the earth: thou shalt not bow down thyself to them, nor serve them: for I the LORD thy God am a jealous God, visiting the iniquity of the fathers upon the children unto the third and fourth generation of them that hate me; and shewing mercy unto thousands of them that love me, and keep my commandments. Thou shalt not take the name of the LORD thy God in vain; for the LORD will not hold him guiltless that taketh his name in vain. Remember the sabbath day, to keep it holy. Six days shalt thou labour, and do all thy work: but the seventh day is the sabbath of the LORD thy God: in it thou shalt not do any work, thou, nor thy son, nor thy daughter, thy manservant, nor thy maidservant, nor thy cattle, nor thy stranger that is within thy gates: for in six days the LORD made heaven and earth, the sea, and all that in them is, and rested the seventh day: wherefore the LORD blessed the sabbath day, and hallowed it. Honour thy father and thy mother: that thy days may be long upon the land which the LORD thy God giveth thee. Thou shalt not kill. Thou shalt not commit adultery. Thou shalt not steal. Thou shalt not bear false witness against thy neighbour. Thou shalt not covet thy neighbour's house, thou shalt not covet thy neighbour's wife, nor

his manservant, nor his maidservant, nor his ox,
nor his ass, nor any thing that is thy neighbour's.

tested by fire

Usage: Refers to a very stringent process of testing;
see also 'baptised by fire'.

Context: Peter encourages believers to see the
difficulties they experience as a process of purification
by which the true value of their faith is proved.
Christians were tortured in Peter's day by the
Roman authorities.

> 1 Peter 1.7
> *that the trial of your faith, being much more*
> *precious than of gold that perisheth, though it be*
> *tried with fire, might be found unto praise and*
> *honour and glory at the appearing of Jesus Christ.*

there is nothing new under the sun

Usage: Whatever people think is new has already
been seen before.

Context: The writer notices that the same patterns
recur in human experience and the life of the world
over and over again.

> Ecclesiastes 1.9
> *The thing that hath been, it is that which shall*
> *be; and that which is done is that which shall be*
> *done: and there is no new thing under the sun.*

thirty pieces of silver

Usage: Represents the price of betrayal.

Context: Judas asks the religious leaders for money
and they agree to pay him to betray Jesus.

> Matthew 26.15
> *and said unto them, What will ye give me, and I*
> *will deliver him unto you? And they covenanted*
> *with him for thirty pieces of silver.*

thorn in the flesh

Usage: A chronic difficulty or problem that dogs
and impedes one.

Context: Paul had an extremely painful physical
condition which kept him humble and reliant on
God. He referred to this as his thorn in the flesh.

> 2 Corinthians 12.7
> *And lest I should be exalted above measure through*
> *the abundance of the revelations, there was given to*
> *me a thorn in the flesh, the messenger of Satan to*
> *buffet me, lest I should be exalted above measure.*

threescore years and ten

Usage: The standard span of an average lifetime referring to 70 years, where a score is 20 years.

Context: In the light of human transience the psalmist urges people to trust in God for lasting benefits.

> **Psalm 90.10**
> *The days of our years are threescore years and ten; And if by reason of strength they be fourscore years, Yet is their strength labour and sorrow; For it is soon cut off, and we fly away.*

through a glass darkly

Usage: Something not quite understood; a sense of the limits of human understanding.

Context: Paul, in his sermon on love, reminds people that their understanding of God is partial. But if they love they understand enough of God to want to know more. The image here may refer to a 'mirror', which in Paul's time distorted rather than gave a perfect image, or to 'glass', which because of impurities in it and uneven surfaces, cut out some of the light.

> **1 Corinthians 13.12**
> *For now we see through a glass, darkly; but then face to face: now I know in part; but then shall I know even as also I am known.*

thy kingdom come

Usage: A line from the Lord's Prayer; 'Till Kingdom Come' is the title of a song by British artists Coldplay, and a line in the song 'Hymn' by Ultravox.

Context: When Jesus taught his disciples a pattern for how to pray to their Father in heaven, he said they should pray to God 'Thy Kingdom come'. The Kingdom was the Kingdom of God, when God would reign in all the world, either spiritually or literally.

> **Matthew 6.10 see also Luke 11.2**
> *Thy kingdom come. Thy will be done in earth, as it is in heaven.*

thy neighbour's wife

Usage: Wanting something you haven't got or can't have.

Context: God's law forbids people desiring things which don't belong to them, such as the wife of a neighbour. It is not advocating that a man should view his wife as a possession.

> **Exodus 20.17**
> *Thou shalt not covet thy neighbour's house, thou shalt not covet thy neighbour's wife, nor his manservant, nor his maidservant, nor his ox, nor his ass, nor any thing that is thy neighbour's.*

tithe

Usage: A tax to support the Church in older times; in some churches the congregation is encouraged to tithe, i.e. 10 per cent of their income.

Context: The people of Israel gave a tenth of their crops to the priests for use in the worship and in support of the religious infrastructure.

> **Leviticus 27.30–32**
> *And all the tithe of the land, whether of the seed of the land, or of the fruit of the tree, is the LORD's: it is holy unto the LORD. And if a man will at all redeem ought of his tithes, he shall add thereto the fifth part thereof. And concerning the tithe of the herd, or of the flock, even of whatsoever passeth under the rod, the tenth shall be holy unto the LORD.*

Tower of Babel

Usage: Synonym of arrogance and confusion.

Context: The Tower of Babel is generally understood to be a huge ziggurat. The ziggurat had a ritual purpose and the building represents both the rebellious pride and the idolatry of the people. God confuses the languages of the people to undermine their aspirations.

> **Genesis 11.1–9**
> *And the whole earth was of one language, and of one speech. And it came to pass, as they journeyed from the east, that they found a plain in the land of Shinar; and they dwelt there. And they said one to another, Go to, let us make brick, and burn them throughly. And they had brick for stone, and slime had they for morter. And they said, Go to, let us build us a city and a tower, whose top may reach unto heaven; and let us make us a name, lest we be scattered abroad upon the face of the whole earth. And the LORD came down to see the city and the tower, which the children of men builded. And the LORD said, Behold, the people is one, and they have all one language; and this they begin to do: and now nothing will be restrained from them, which they have imagined to do. Go to, let us go down, and there confound their language, that they may not understand one another's speech. So the LORD scattered them abroad from thence upon the face of all the earth: and they left off to build the city. Therefore is the name of it called Babel; because the LORD did there confound the language of all the earth: and from thence did the LORD scatter them abroad upon the face of all the earth.*

train up a child in the way he should go and when he is grown he will not depart from it

Usage: The lessons of childhood result in future right living.

Context: The things taught to a child are those things that become habits and build character.

> **Proverbs 22.6**
> *Train up a child in the way he should go: And when he is old, he will not depart from it.*

treasure in clay pots / earthen vessels

Usage: A synonym for hidden value in the guise of ordinary things.

Context: Paul recognises that while Christians have been given all the riches of God's grace they, nevertheless, are still human and fallible.

> **2 Corinthians 4.7**
> *But we have this treasure in earthen vessels, that the excellency of the power may be of God, and not of us.*

turn the other cheek

Usage: Refuse to react angrily.

Context: Jesus asks his followers to be willing to suffer for him, even to the point of letting people strike them not just once, but again and again. He demands they do more than what was agreed to be conventionally good.

> **Matthew 5.39 see also Luke 6.29**
> *but I say unto you, That ye resist not evil: but whosoever shall smite thee on thy right cheek, turn to him the other also.*

twinkling of an eye

Usage: A split second.

Context: Paul teaches that Jesus' return is not to be understood as a process but the end of time. There will be no time for reflection, but rather the truth about who we are will suddenly and finally be revealed.

> **1 Corinthians 15.52**
> *in a moment, in the twinkling of an eye, at the last trump: for the trumpet shall sound, and the dead shall be raised incorruptible, and we shall be changed.*

under the sun

Usage: Refers to the world, or on Earth; it is particularly common in the phrase 'nothing new under the sun' which is used to mean everything has already been seen, or done, before; the title of a song by Black Sabbath (1972).

Context: Under the sun is a Hebrew idiom which is used 29 times in the book of Ecclesiastes, referring to the people and places that the sun shines upon. According to Jewish rabbinic tradition, the point of Ecclesiastes is to state that all is futile under the sun. One should therefore ignore physical pleasures and put all one's efforts towards that which is above the Sun, i.e. heaven.

Ecclesiastes 1.9
The thing that hath been, it is that which shall be; and that which is done is that which shall be done: and there is no new thing under the sun.

valley of the shadow of death

Usage: Often refers to severe adversity or depression.

Context: Psalm 23 appears to refer to darkness like death is imagined to be; the very deepest darkness.

Psalm 23.4
Yea, though I walk through the valley of the shadow of death, I will fear no evil: for thou art with me; Thy rod and thy staff they comfort me.

vanity of vanities

Usage: Pointlessness, though in recent expression it seems also to refer to vanity in the sense of being concerned about one's appearance.

Context: The book of Ecclesiastes is an experiment in pretending God does not exist: when viewed from this perspective, life is supremely pointless and an exercise in attempting to please oneself.

Ecclesiastes 1.2
Vanity of vanities, saith the Preacher, vanity of vanities; all is vanity.

vengeance is mine (I will repay says the Lord)

Usage: In the face of provocation, leave punishment of the wrongdoer to God. Sometimes the first part of the saying is misappropriated by people who wish to exact their own revenge.

Context: Paul warns Christians against vengefulness: it is God's prerogative alone.

Romans 12.19
Dearly beloved, avenge not yourselves, but rather give place unto wrath: for it is written, Vengeance is mine; I will repay, saith the Lord.

voice crying in the wilderness

Usage: Used of someone with foresight who is not listened to.

Context: When God visits and restores his people, a great road will lead to the New Jerusalem fit for a king to travel on. In the Gospels, John the Baptist is seen as the voice who calls out to announce the king's (Jesus') arrival.

> **Isaiah 40.3**
> *The voice of him that crieth in the wilderness, Prepare ye the way of the LORD, make straight in the desert a highway for our God.*

wages of sin is death

Usage: Bad consequences follow wrongdoing.

Context: Paul argues that going against God inevitably brings its own reward: death. But God generously offers the gift of life through Christ. And thus he urges Christians to live in God's gift rather than the ways of sin.

> **Romans 6.23**
> *For the wages of sin is death; but the gift of God is eternal life through Jesus Christ our Lord.*

washing one's hands of something

Usage: To deny any responsibility for something or someone.

Context: Pilate gives in to the crowd's demand that Jesus be crucified even though he knows Jesus to be innocent. The hand-washing is a symbolic action, removing the stain of blood that the people's decision will bring.

> **Matthew 27.24**
> *When Pilate saw that he could prevail nothing, but that rather a tumult was made, he took water, and washed his hands before the multitude, saying, I am innocent of the blood of this just person: see ye to it.*

watch in the night

Usage: A brief period of time.

Context: The psalmist contrasts the eternal nature of God with the transient nature of humanity. A thousand years is but a blink of an eye for God. A watch was a third of the night or four hours, depending on the length of the night.

> **Psalm 90.4**
> *For a thousand years in thy sight are but as yesterday When it is past, and as a watch in the night.*

weaker vessel

Usage: Synonym for a woman, often used ironically.

Context: In the ancient world women were thought to be less physically and mentally strong than men. Peter reminds men that God has given both sexes the grace of life.

1 Peter 3.7
Likewise, ye husbands, dwell with them according to knowledge, giving honour unto the wife, as unto the weaker vessel, and as being heirs together of the grace of life; that your prayers be not hindered.

weighed in the balance

Usage: Used when actions / lives are being assessed and judgement passed.

Context: At Belshazzar's feast a mysterious finger writes on the wall what amounts to a judgement on the king. He has been tested and has failed the test.

Daniel 5.27
Thou art weighed in the balances, and art found wanting.

well done good and faithful servant

Usage: Praise for someone who has undertaken a task successfully.

Context: In the parable of the talents, the master praises his servants for making use of the money he gave them; Christians hope to hear Jesus saying these words to those when they are welcomed into heaven.

Matthew 25.21
His lord said unto him, Well done, thou good and faithful servant: thou hast been faithful over a few things, I will make thee ruler over many things: enter thou into the joy of thy lord.

what God hath joined together let no man put asunder

Usage: The part of the traditional Christian marriage ceremony that states God's authority over man.

Context: Jesus uses the term when talking to the Pharisees in answer to the question about the validity of divorce.

Matthew 19.6
Wherefore they are no more twain, but one flesh. What therefore God hath joined together, let not man put asunder.

wheat and tares

Usage: Good and bad people or situations; see also 'sheep and goats'.

Context: In the parable, an enemy has sown a weed that looks like wheat in its early growth in the farmer's field. The servants want to pull it up so that the wheat can grow. But the master tells them to leave it until the harvest. The field represents the world and the harvest represents the last judgement as commonly interpreted.

Matthew 13.30
Let both grow together until the harvest: and in the time of harvest I will say to the reapers, Gather ye together first the tares, and bind them in bundles to burn them: but gather the wheat into my barn.

whited sepulchre

Usage: Or whitened sepulchre or whitewashed tomb; a hypocrite.

Context: Tombs painted on the outside look pretty but they merely disguise death and decay. It refers to the tombs on the Mount of Olives where righteous Jews sought to be buried, so that in the final resurrection they faced the Temple.

Matthew 23.27
Woe unto you, scribes and Pharisees, hypocrites! for ye are like unto whited sepulchres, which indeed appear beautiful outward, but are within full of dead men's bones, and of all uncleanness.

whitewashed wall

Usage: A hypocrite.

Context: Paul angrily responds to being unlawfully struck on the mouth. His accusation against the High Priest's action is justified as the High Priest needs to act justly yet is himself disobeying the law.

Acts 23.3
Then said Paul unto him, God shall smite thee, thou whited wall: for sittest thou to judge me after the law, and commandest me to be smitten contrary to the law?

whole duty of man

Usage: Everything expected of a human.

Context: A summary of and response to the search for meaning in life in Ecclesiastes, which is essentially to obey God's guidance for human life.

Ecclesiastes 12.13
Let us hear the conclusion of the whole matter: Fear God, and keep his commandments: for this is the whole duty of man.

widow's mite

Usage: A tiny amount of money which is, nevertheless, significant.

Context: Jesus praises a widow for her self-sacrificial giving as it is a huge proportion of her income. Those more wealthy were giving much more in monetary terms, but only a fraction of their total wealth.

> **Mark 12.42**
> *And there came a certain poor widow, and she threw in two mites, which make a farthing.*

wisdom of Solomon

Usage: Outstanding insight.

Context: Solomon became a byword for wisdom. The authorship of Proverbs, Ecclesiastes and the Song of Solomon in the Bible is attributed to him.

> **1 Kings 4.29–31 see also Proverbs**
> *And God gave Solomon wisdom and understanding exceeding much, and largeness of heart, even as the sand that is on the sea shore. And Solomon's wisdom excelled the wisdom of all the children of the east country, and all the wisdom of Egypt. For he was wiser than all men; than Ethan the Ezrahite, and Heman, and Chalcol, and Darda, the sons of Mahol: and his fame was in all nations round about.*

woe is me

Usage: Used as a saying when someone is distressed, sad or grieved; used by Shakespeare in *Hamlet*.

Context: Forms of this phrase occur many times in the Bible, where the writers bemoan their circumstances.

> **Job 10.15 see also Psalm 120.5; Isaiah 6.5; Jeremiah 4.31**
> *If I be wicked, woe unto me; And if I be righteous, yet will I not lift up my head. I am full of confusion; Therefore see thou mine affliction;*

wolf in sheep's clothing

Usage: Someone who pretends to be a friend but is not.

Context: The false prophets look like teachers and preachers of Christ but if their teaching is false and aims at gratifying the prophets it will destroy God's flock.

> **Matthew 7.15**
> *Beware of false prophets, which come to you in sheep's clothing, but inwardly they are ravening wolves.*

working out one's own salvation

Usage: Getting oneself out of a mess.

Context: Paul urges the Philippians to see that God inspires their Christian service. God works with them as they do what he requires.

Philippians 2.12–13
Wherefore, my beloved, as ye have always obeyed, not as in my presence only, but now much more in my absence, work out your own salvation with fear and trembling. For it is God which worketh in you both to will and to do of his good pleasure.

writing on the wall

Usage: A dire warning of the end of something.

Context: At Belshazzar's feast a mysterious finger writes on the wall what amounts to a judgement on the king. The king is frightened and with good reason: that night he dies.

Daniel 5.5
In the same hour came forth fingers of a man's hand, and wrote over against the candlestick upon the plaister of the wall of the king's palace: and the king saw the part of the hand that wrote.

your sin will find you out

Usage: You can't hide what you have done forever.

Context: Moses agrees to the request of the tribes of Reuben and Gad to settle on the safe side of the River Jordan. But he warns them that if they ignore the call to serve in the army when they go in to conquer the land of Canaan, that will be sin against God and will be punished by him.

Numbers 32.23
But if ye will not do so, behold, ye have sinned against the Lord: and be sure your sin will find you out.